THE VISITOR

THE
VISITOR

Jack Hayford

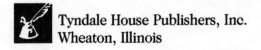

Tyndale House Publishers, Inc.
Wheaton, Illinois

All Bible verses are from *The Holy Bible,* New King
James Version (NKJV), copyright 1982 by Thomas
Nelson, Inc., unless otherwise noted as being from
The Living Bible, copyright 1971 by Tyndale House
Publishers.

Front cover illustration by Nathan Greene

First printing, November 1986

Library of Congress Catalog Card Number 86-51157
ISBN 0-8423-7802-2, paper
ISBN 0-8423-7814-6, cloth
Copyright 1986 by Jack Hayford
All rights reserved
Printed in the United States of America

CONTENTS

INTRODUCTION

Death or dynamic? Of which does Christ's suffering speak to you?

I want to affirm its dynamism because there *is* dynamic in an uncluttered insight into the suffering of Christ.

Religious forms in art and practice tend to reduce any remembrance of Christ's suffering to maudlin mourning. A pitiful, regret-filled, if not weepy exercise in pointlessness too often ensues. One would surmise that some goal of godliness was being proposed—that God would be especially delighted if we would all "feel worse about Jesus' dying," as though the quest for spirituality is a contest in contrition.

But would you please, just for a moment, feature yourself in Jesus' place? Do you see Him as self-pitying? Can you even imagine Him saying, "I wish you would be more despondent when you think of everything I did for you. You know, it really hurt a lot!"

Such a caricature is virtual sacrilege, certainly unrepresentative of the Christ we see during His lifetime, and even less representative of the Christ we now meet enthroned in

His triumph. We can no more imagine Jesus being "pathetic" than we can imagine any psychologically healthy person wanting people to "feel bad for him." No! Jesus isn't pitiful or self-pitying. But it can add to our blessing and wisdom to understand His suffering, because He experienced it all for very real purposes—purposes that can be applied to the practical outworking of our lives today.

I would like to invite you to join me in thinking through Christ's sufferings: His wounds, His blood, . . . and His death. In looking at these facts, I'm hoping we will better capture the meaning of all He came to do for us, and the power He wants to give us today through it all.

There is power here that could never come from a self-inflicted spirit of mourning. It is a power born of a Holy Spirit-anointed perspective—of an insight into how and why Jesus suffered and what it accomplished. Only then can we learn to receive His provision and to participate in it with understanding.

Jesus said, "If I do not go to the Father, the Spirit cannot come to you." We know well His remarkable life; if His death makes way for that life to be available to any who thirst after it, is that not dynamic?

"He is not dead! He is risen, as He said!"; and what that means to us is the greatest and most powerful miracle of all.

PART ONE

THE
VISITOR

In the sight of the unwise they seemed to die; . . . but in the time of their visitation they shall shine, and run to and fro like sparks among the stubble. (The Wisdom of Solomon 2:3, 7, *The Apocrypha*)

HOW LONG THE NIGHT

The Day is sure; the night will fade.
The harvest—tho' it seems delayed—
will surely come.
My eyes shall see it, all around,
the light, the wheat upon the ground.
When morning comes,
When harvest comes,
My eyes shall see.

J. W. H.

Therefore we must give the more earnest heed to the things we have heard, lest we drift away. For if the word spoken through angels proved steadfast, and every transgression and disobedience received a just reward, how shall we escape if we neglect so great a salvation, which at the first began to be spoken by the Lord, and was confirmed to us by those who heard Him, God also bearing witness both with signs and wonders, with various miracles, and gifts of the Holy Spirit, according to His own will?

For He has not put the world to come, of which we speak, in

subjection to angels. But one testified in a certain place, saying:

"What is man that You are mindful of him, or the son of man that You take care of him? You made him a little lower than the angels; You crowned him with glory and honor, and set him over the works of Your hands. You have put all things in subjection under his feet."

For in that He put all in subjection under him, He left nothing that is not put under him. But now we do not yet see all things put under him. But we see Jesus, who was made a little lower than the angels, for the suffering of death crowned with glory and honor, that He, by the grace of God, might taste death for everyone. (Hebrews 2:1-9)

ONE
THE COMING
OF THE VISITOR

How wonderful to receive a timely visit from a welcomed friend! We've all been pleasantly surprised by a visitor—by someone arriving at just the right time. (We have also experienced the exact opposite: the awkwardness in the arrival of an unexpected guest when everything's a mess!) And how many of us have known the loneliness and disappointment of having been forgotten, left alone . . . when no one came at all.

Both the positive and negative remembrances of such experiences heighten our sense of the significance of having a visitor. And we begin here, because the focus of our text is on the fact that God became a visitor . . . that He came to visit us—mankind.

The older English version of the Bible reads, "What is man . . . that thou visitest him?" All the richness of the words—visit, visitor, visitation—are wrapped in *episkeptomai,* the poignant Greek verb used here. The idea is one of caring; caring so much that one makes a point to come to beloved friends to visit them—much as a gentle family physician would make a house call. And this is exactly what we are being told by the Scriptures: God became a visitor to mankind, and in His coming man experienced a "visitation."

Let us think about this tender truth and all it entails: God has visited us.

THE REASON FOR THE VISIT

"What is man that You are mindful of him, and the son of man that You visit him?" (Ps. 8:4).

These words are taken from a psalm in which David relates his awe as he observes the midnight sky. Studying its star-spangled beauty, he says, "God, when I look at the vastness of space and the marvel of creation around me, I say, 'Why do you even bother with man? And still, you've crowned him with glory and honor. You've given him dominion over the works of your hands!'"

The Scriptures repeatedly assert man's significance in the divine design amid the cosmic order of things. In contrast, however, we too often confine our thinking to the opening words, "What is man?" On the tongue of the unknowing, that question may span the spectrum from an honest-hearted inquiry to a cynical epithet spat in scorn. One may honestly wonder what man's purpose could be, while another may defiantly challenge any presumption of "purpose." Any of us may too readily allow ourself to be reduced to the proposition, "If there is a God, then how arrogant man is in supposing himself to be of significance amidst the sprawling cosmos of that God's awesome creation."

"I mean, after all," doubt argues, "what are we but an advanced collection of cells in constant chemical transition, objects destined at best for survival of the fittest, at worst for pointless extinction? How dare we propose 'divine intent' in our evolving, we whose backaches testify to our animal descent? Here we are, barely able to stand upright, occupying an insignificant planet and presumptuously talking about ruling the universe!"

"Best admit it," the scoffer insists. "Our only role is to survive on this third rock from the sun, in a galaxy that is but one among billions spinning randomly through a measureless universe!"

But a stark rebuttal to such human doubt and scoffing appears in our text. Man's worth and destiny are asserted in God's Word. At the heart of God's purpose in providing man's redemption is this lofty truth: He has a cosmic intention in man's creation, and His coming to visit man is key to that intent being realized. Our emphasis on the Bible's declaration of a phenomenal destiny for man is not an empty effort at ego gratification, but a simple exercise in honesty before God's Word. To see this in His Word is to see why He was willing to pay so exorbitant a price to regain mankind; a price that begins with His stooping to earth, condescending to *come* and revealing above all a love that cared enough to pay a "visit."

The scenario unfolds in the Bible's opening chapters. Almighty God is forced to deal with a crisis regarding His beloved creature, Man. Man has breached a divinely endowed trust. Because of this, he has suffered a loss which can only be reinstated to the Creator's intended order by His loving

13

initiative. The distance between the exalted God and the broken race of man can only be spanned from the Deity's side.

And He does it. He chooses to come. He chooses to care. And it is before this awesome fact that the psalmist marvels, "My God, what a wonder! What must You have in mind for mankind that You should visit him?"

What is a visitor? Visitors come for a variety of reasons. A visitor may come when someone is sick, or he may come to assist somehow when help is needed. One visitor may simply come to show friendliness, while another's arrival may be to give comfort when someone has died.

A visitor's presence could signal that someone needs tutoring, a time having been set for the lesson: "Shall we say once a week at four o'clock, on Thursday afternoon? Fine. Your piano teacher will be there."

A visitor may come simply to make an acquaintance: "Hello. We noticed you just moved in a few days ago. We live next door, and just came over to introduce ourselves and to welcome you."

Visitors come when people are hungry or needy. "We're from the social welfare agency. We've been advised there is need here, and we have provisions available for your family if you'd like them."

Or a visitor may come for simpler, more sentimental reasons. All our hearts are warmed when someone arrives or calls just to say, "I came by today simply to tell you I love you."

Ah, we need that. A visit "just because" somebody loves us!

Visitors also come at painful times. The telephone rings: "You had better come quickly, he's weakening. There isn't much time left—at least in this world." And against apparent hopelessness, the visit is made. Relatives fly in from all parts of the nation, hoping for one last opportunity to see a loved one.

This is why visits are made: because people care about each other. And considering all of the above reasons can deepen our appreciation for that occasion when the Lord— God Himself—came to visit us. For His coming was in the style of all of the aforementioned situations.

Someone had died—a race had lost its living relationship with God. And since the death-plague infected our whole race, He came to visit us in our sickness.

And there was need—hungry people everywhere, then as today. And beyond his immediate need of bread for his body, man's soul still clamors for something to satisfy his deepest hunger. Covetousness goads him—the need to have—and it breeds an appetite for emptiness. An unending lust for "more" tugs at us all and, like the prodigal son, we too often end our quest in a pigsty.

It is difficult to criticize the sinning that results from this human hunger—the need to have. Most who sin do so more from desperation than out of conscious disobedience. Their sinning is not so much because of intended rebellion as it is because of blind hunger—not knowing where to find Life-Bread. This is why the Visitor came saying, "I have brought,

15

indeed, *I Am*, that Bread of Life, the answer to your hunger" (see John 6:48-51).

This holy Visitor also came to establish acquaintance: "You can know the Living God . . . truly know Him personally. I have come to show you the Father."

If ever a teacher came to visit, this is the one. He came to teach us clearly what the Father is like. "If you've seen Me, you have seen the Father," He says to those He visits. (See John 14:6-11; Col. 1:19; 2:9.) Jesus is the precise revelation of Father God's nature, in contrast to the images which human imagination sometimes projects! Distorted images of "father" often haunt us; humanly fallible authority figures sour our view of God. But shedding His light and dispelling the shadows of confusion, Jesus visits us to show how the eternal Father expresses authority and love in equal balance. We see the complete reality of God in this Visitor, for "in Him dwells all the fullness of God" (Col. 2:9, author's paraphrase).

Our Visitor also came just to say, "I love you." It is perfectly appropriate simply to look into His face and let the full measure of His words touch your emotions. He does love you.

Deeply.

And thoroughly.

And unless we gain a deep sense of that love, we are going to miss more than we can possibly imagine.

See Jesus as He weeps over Jerusalem, saying, "The day of your visitation has come and you didn't recognize it." (See Luke 19:42.) Those words clarify our need for and our wisdom in firmly grasping and thoroughly understanding this fact: We have been visited. Let those words sink into your soul, for no matter what you face, the Visitor is there, bringing a power that can flow to you now because of the visit He made long ago. For you see, He has, in that one grand visit, already accomplished whatever today's or tomorrow's need may demand! And now, God's Holy Spirit has come to interpret for and ignite in us all that is available to us. Because of Christ's condescendence—His coming to visit us—we can not only survive the stress and personal failure of trials, but we can be restored to His highest purposes for us.

Speak it aloud.

Declare it now: "I have been visited! Praise You, Lord! I marvel at Your loving purpose for me—that, in order to assure its fulfillment, You have paid me a visit."

And while you're praising Him for that, further thank Him that He has also promised to abide with you forever.

Never leaving.

Never forsaking.

TWO
THE PROBLEMS
IN THE VISIT

A visit was needed.

Mankind needed God's care and help. But there was another need, and it is important that we study that need to gain a complete understanding and appreciation of the visit.

The other need was the Visitor's.

If someone is going to pay a visit, then there are difficulties which may not be apparent to us but which the visitor knows he must resolve. What is obvious to us is that anyone who is going to pay a visit will need to give a certain amount of time and effort to go to the place of his visit. Unless these demands are met, neither the visit, nor the benefits of the visit, are possible.

A telephone conversation may allow us to share and talk with others, but when someone can and actually does come to visit us, we value the investment—the time and energy given to more fully understand our situation and genuinely care for us. And so it was that giving time and going personally were the essential requirements that our heavenly Visitor had to meet, both for His purposes and for our needs.

But here is a problem: In this Visitor's need to go to a specific place and spend a given amount of time, there are difficulties that go beyond the inconveniences a human visitor must overcome. This heavenly Visitor faces confining factors that are contrary to His very being.

Since the One who is giving time and going on a personal visit is God Himself, we are confronted with enormous difficulties that are rooted in God's very nature. First, we are speaking of the Eternal One giving time—but God is timeless. Second, we are speaking of the Omnipresent One going to one place, on a solitary planet—but God is everywhere!

These seeming contradictions defy easy analysis and exceed our general suppositions, because human concepts of God usually are too small. We tend to think of Him on human terms within human definitions that haven't been sufficiently expanded to include His full "God-ness." God is not simply a larger-than-life humanoid. He strongly asserts this in His Word, emphasizing the contrast between man's limitations and fallibility and God's transcendency and perfection:

"For as the heavens are higher than the earth, so are My ways higher than your ways, and My thoughts than your thoughts" (Isa. 55:9).

"God is not a man, that He should lie" (Num. 23:19).

"As for the Almighty, we cannot find Him; He is excellent in power, in judgment and abundant justice; He does not oppress" (Job 37:23).

God is not manlike; not even *super*manlike. He clearly states that He is wholly "other" from us—on another plane entirely. And though that should humble us, He doesn't say it to humiliate us. Nor does He declare His exceeding difference from us to make us grovel before His throne. But we must see something of these dimensions of His greatness to fully appreciate the investment He makes in visiting us. Here is the Eternal One planning to give us time; the Omnipresent One preparing to confine Himself to one place; and the Omniscient One who, knowing all things, still comes to learn of life on the terms of His own creation. This condescension is not easily accomplished.

GOD WITHIN TIME

To understand the problems inherent in God's confinement of Himself to time, we have to think clearly about eternity. Too many view eternity from a linear perspective, as though it is only the sum of the indefinite past and the infinite future. But to do this is to omit the present. Human reason tends to separate "eternity" from the present era of human experience; somehow trying to crowd human history into a parenthesis between two eternities—"the eternal past and the eternal future."

From such a limited perspective, eternity is both unreal and irrelevant; a philosophical blind spot that puts the todays of our lives in a space between the two eternities, yet insulated from them. By such reasoning, today becomes a temporary zone—aside and apart from the eternal—where our daily existence occurs. But time and eternity should not be confused by such compartmentalizing, as though time refers only to where I live now, and eternity refers to something either remotely past or distantly future.

The truth of God's Word is that time—our present moment—is an immediate part of eternity: eternity in *now.* Eternity encompasses time as an ocean encompasses a water drop. All that ocean's drops are ever-present, they are now. From God's eternity perspective, both the future and the past are now. They are occurring in ongoing process. That is why Christ is called the Alpha and the Omega—the beginning and the ending—for by His eternal nature He encompasses everything before time, of time, and beyond time.

But this is not so with us. Mankind is locked in a time-space continuum, limited to this immediate moment—just now, today, this instant. We are always looking back to the before or forward to the after. And yet our present is not excluded, isolated, or separate from eternity, it is *within* it. We are within eternity, but not beyond it. God is both. He fills eternity and exists above and beyond it. He fills all time, including each present moment, while at the same time infinitely transcending it. And it is this transcendent quality of His eternal nature that brings one of our Visitor's problems into focus.

If God, who has no limitations, is to visit people who are locked into the limits of time, how is He going to confine Himself only to "now"—to time? He can do so only if He will consent to a proposition which, by reason of His nature as eternal, is a step of incredible, incalculable condescension. He must restrict Himself to a time segment. In doing so, He must somehow temporarily set aside the aspect of His being which we call "eternal." So the Second Person of the Godhead—Jesus the Son—accepts the restriction of a thirty-three-earth-year time measure to accomplish this visit! How can we help but be humbled by this Visitor's willingness? Why, when He can create a galaxy by merely speaking a word, would He stoop to the limits of time to do His work? Why not accomplish man's salvation in an instant—with a word or a momentary action?

Why?

Because without time, without a season spent in visiting, He would neither gain the confidence of nor experience the full identification with the ones He seeks to save—mankind. And mankind needed time to know Him. So He chose to take time to be with them, and in that choice the Visitor allowed His eternal being to be temporarily walled within the restrictions of time.

GOD WITHIN SPACE

Secondly, for the Omnipresent One to come and be with us, the visited ones, He had to become visible and touchable. He could not simply say, "I am everywhere, so reach out—I'm there." He can and does say this after His coming, but to first establish contact the Visitor had to visit us on terms we could see and understand. He who fills the heavens stooped to earth. He who can span the universe faster than the speed of light was willingly limited to the pace at which human feet tread earth's dusty roads. The people He had chosen to visit could not fathom "omnipresence," nor could they touch "spirit." So, the Visitor willingly confined Himself in terms of space . . . to come to us.

Within these limits of time and space, He also accepted additional terms. In consenting to visit us, Christ placed

23

Omniscience into the schoolroom of human experience. He who knows all acknowledged His desire to learn, to discover human pain in a human body, to feel human disappointment with human emotions, and to suffer human misunderstanding. He might simply have asserted His perception of these human sensations. His justice would have been no less righteous. He would not have been less loving, less holy or less God had He never submitted to these things. But He *did* submit. And in coming, He accepted these restrictions: "Though He was a Son, yet He learned obedience by the things which He suffered" (Heb. 5:8).

No wonder the psalmist marvels, "What is man that You visit him?"

The Eternal One confined Himself to time.

The Omnipresent One confined Himself to one place.

The Omniscient One chose to learn the frailty of humanity.

THREE
WHO IS THIS VISITOR?

The One who would make this visit, who would go through this condescension, is named in Hebrews 2:9: "But we see Jesus, who was made a little lower than the angels." In those few words we are given the fact of Jesus' condescension. The word *condescension* could be objectionable to some. It can sound as though God were patronizing man. We must avoid the ignorance or presumption of such objections, and a precise assessment of who the Visitor is will help us do that. When we see more completely the uniqueness of His nature we will be better equipped to escape the potential arrogance which entraps those ingrained with pagan philosophy or humanistic theology.

MAN-SIZED IDEAS AREN'T ENOUGH
Pagan and popular ideas about God are everywhere. As in the ancient *Odyssey* and the *Illiad*, "pop" views of God are heard today, notions which reduce Him to little more than an oversized human. In varied ways, God is recast in twentieth-century terms—from the hip "Big Daddy" to the depersonalized "Force." This is little more than verbal re-

tooling of the characters in the legends of Greece, Rome, or Scandinavia, where "gods" were merely immortal men with superhuman powers. They remain humanly unpredictable, moody, immoral and vindictive—with one twist. Being immortal and having virtually unlimited power, they rule in might—unjust, vengeful, and brutal. This broadly defines the average man's view of God today—even if that "god" is only called "Fate."

Careless thinking and general ignorance introduce so many distorted views of the living God that it is a small wonder that so many prefer agnosticism or atheism—denying God's existence outright. It seems a sounder option than to believe in a God defined by humanized theology. Cheap theology breeds unbelief, and one cannot blame the person who does not believe in a God like that.

I wouldn't either.

But to think clearly of Jesus—the One made lower than angels—we must understand something of the dimension of His nature before He was made lower. This perspective builds a faith which senses man's high destiny and purpose, since it perceives the true dimension of the Person who came. When we see the full glory of the person of Jesus, we begin to see what it was worth to Him to pay mankind a visit; not to mention what man was worth to God that He would extend and expend the life of His Son.

Hebrews 1:1-3 introduces us to several facets of the glory of this Visitor:

> God, who at various times and in different ways spoke
> in time past to the fathers by the prophets, has in these

last days spoken to us by His Son, whom He has appointed heir of all things, through whom also He made the worlds; who being the brightness of His glory and the express image of His person, and upholding all things by the word of His power, when He had by Himself purged our sins, sat down at the right hand of the Majesty on high.

These verses declare that God has conclusively spoken to us through His Son. Jesus Christ *is* God's message to man. Jesus is not only a message of God's love, but He communicates God's likeness—that is, what He is really like. A careful summary of His attributes is important to help us form our perceptions of the Visitor, His interest in us, and the worth He places upon us.

First, He is "heir of all things." It has pleased God that all things will ultimately dwell in Christ—that everything in creation will ultimately belong to Him. No stipulations are made as to the requirements He must meet to receive this. The visit isn't demanded—only requested. This One, volunteering to bear all the humbling confinements the visit requires, is the One to whom all things have already been promised: "It is my will," the Father has said, "that all the cosmos be His—My Son's." So why then this remarkable condescension? The staggering truth is that it is for one reason: *His visit is in our interest to allow for the possibility that we—you and I—might share with Him in that cosmic inheritance* (see Rom. 8:15-23)!

Second, He made all things: "Through whom also He made the worlds." The partnership within the Trinity at

27

creation is an interesting study: God willed all things to be, the Son spoke all things into existence as the Father willed, and the Holy Spirit's power was the energy by which all things were brought into being. Creation is the product of the Father's will, the Son's word, and the Spirit's work.

> Before anything else existed, there was Christ, with God. He has always been alive and is Himself God. He created everything there is—nothing exists that he didn't make. (John 1:1-3, TLB)

Let it not escape our understanding: the Visitor was present at the founding of creation, yet He chose to become a part of it Himself.

Third, He is the express image of God. The Greek noun *karakter* (image) was commonly used in the ancient world to describe the figure struck on a coin when minted. By its engraved authenticity and its stamped value a coin declares its worth and its genuineness. And so it is with Jesus, for when we look at Him we are seeing the full worthiness and the true magnificence of God. In Christ, all confusion as to what God is like is cleared up. Jesus is His "express image," indeed the genuine article—the Son of the God above all gods. He is not a fluke of humanity or a human with divine genius. He is divine in His entirety, notwithstanding His having adopted man's humanity with all its limits, except for sin.

Fourth, He upholds all things by the word of His power. This is to say that He who spoke all things into existence continues by the sheer power of His creative word to sustain them in existence. Thus, the authority and the almightiness invested in the words our Visitor speaks will be of another quality. When He speaks a promise, it can be believed. When He declares a goal concerning His work and His will for His own redeemed, we can depend on His bringing it about. Loved one, if He can sustain all creation by His own word, we can rest assured He'll see us through when He says He will! Hallelujah!

Fifth, He "by Himself purged our sins." "By Himself" means both alone and without need of added worth. He made Himself the price for our sins, pouring out His own blood. Further, the value of this payment is sufficient to satisfy the immeasurable, incredible debt of human sin. And it is because of this sufficiency that these words are spoken: "He sat down at the right hand of the Majesty on high." When He does this, He is making a divine announcement that, "My work is done—it is finished." The high quality, the peerless character, and the eternal significance of our Visitor all are shown in the completion of His assignment. Upon His finishing with that task, having visited us in a form "a little lower than the angels," He returns to be with His Father on high.

But during that visit, He was killed.

The process, simply stated in the phrase, "when He had by Himself purged our sins," involved His death. He submitted to it—willingly. He came to accomplish it. It was included in the visitation plans.

But man didn't know of that willingness or of that plan.

He only functioned in the limits of his own blindness, bondage, and capacity for folly. And so it was that we killed the Visitor . . . this One of eternal, regal, noble stature. And He refused retaliation, for He had accomplished the high objective of His coming—He had visited us with salvation.

FOUR
INQUIRING INTO THE
UNFATHOMABLE

Now of this Visitor mankind killed, we are flatly told, "[He was made] a little lower than the angels" (Heb. 2:9).

This brings us to the most difficult point in attempting to understand His coming. First, there is the staggering truth of such condescension in itself—God, lower than His own creatures. But even more, we are overwhelmed by the fact that we have no point of reference as to the degree of stooping or condescending this represents. What is the distance from God to angels, or from angels to man? There are no hints in the Bible, so how can we measure positional distances between the roles or ranks of creatures? We are placed in the position of inquiring into the unfathomable . . . the measureless expanse between the persons of God and man.

To begin, the one thing we can readily understand is that there is a vast difference between the Creator and His creation. For example, I know the man who built the pulpit from which I teach and preach. It's a very fine demonstration of my friend's craftsmanship. It tells you something of his skill and creativity, but there is no real comparison between the artisan and the lectern; there is an immeasurable difference and distance between the man and his work. If he were to stand alongside his handiwork, who could draw a valid assessment of the relative worth of either man or pulpit?

So when we begin with the Creator of *all* things, and attempt to measure the space between His being and His creation, there seems to be no way to comprehend the distance. And in our seeing Jesus made a little lower than the angels, we face the same dilemma. There seems to be no point of reference or comparison; no mathematics, economics, or geometrics exist for us to even begin to develop an appreciation of the vast distance God spanned when He became man.

A FOUNDATION FOR VALUES

This problem deserves our attention, for we are dealing with more than speculation about the grandeur of God from man's viewpoint. We are also dealing with the value of man from God's perspective. Our inability to precisely, intelligently assess God's greatness also peculiarly inhibits our ability to place a proper value on ourselves; and it is precisely that value, which He saw in us, that caused Him to span that cosmic chasm to pay us the visit.

That consideration is important to us, not for self-congratulation or a contrived inflation of our human worth, but so that an accurate evaluation of man's potential and prospective purpose might be made. God spanned the universe that separated us from Him not to capture a pawn, but *to win a race of kings.*

This will alter a person's viewpoint on the greatness of God's salvation, which is an indispensable need for any who have a smaller perspective on the nature of the Visitor or on the magnitude of His condescension.

Intelligently understanding. Truly understanding and appreciating "so great a salvation" provides real grounds for our placing a value on man—the object of God's visit. This standard of evaluating human worth excels the best effort of humanistic philosophy, which must depend upon its own self-assessment to establish values. Man's philosophical base is a closed system which imposes severe limits that reduce man's intrinsic value; at best, cheapening him, and at worst, obliterating his purpose and destiny.

At best, humanized systems make man out to be an ascending god with virtually unlimited inherent potential for becoming. But this view cheapens man's actual worth because while it affirms those possibilities it provides no better leverage than man himself to accomplish them. Age upon age has already verified the inability of human flesh to catapult man into his new age of self-realization. Thus, this proposition insults human intelligence by attempting to sell philosophical froth again and again.

At worst, human systems cast man as either an advanced animal or a sophisticated mixture of chemicals boiled to a new stage of attainment intellectually, sociologically, and technologically. This view obliterates man's highest destiny, for it proposes nothing of spirit transcending the drive of an animal, and nothing of timelessness exceeding the durability of inert matter. It is only when such static states of thought are confronted and corrected by the revelation of God's Word and truth in Christ that human values are most intelligently understood and that man's highest potential and eternal destiny are realized.

Our investigation then—our inquiry into the unfathomable—is for practical reasons. A deepened understanding of Christ's condescension will increase our sense of man's distinct destiny and our present purpose. Such dynamic faith, born of clear-headed insight into eternal issues, will begin to alter our priorities.

Praise toward God will increase!

Self-esteem can rise!

The spirit of faith will soar!

All of this flows from the uplifting certainty that the One who has reached so far to touch me is certainly not going to fail me now. He is absolutely committed to seeing me through to the full realization of His purpose for my existence.

Two questions to resolve. Increasing our realization of God's purpose will be easier if we resolve two points: (1) Why was He made lower than angels? and (2) Can we conceive of the reality that this did, indeed, happen?

First, *why* was He made lower than angels? The answer is direct and absolute: It was planned so that He could experience suffering and death. Unless He becomes a man, He cannot do either. There is no other way to pay the price of salvation, no other way to release mankind at every point of his bondage. We will examine these details further, but it is enough for now to say it all had to take place on these terms and in human flesh.

Secondly, *can* we conceive of the reality that Christ was "made a little lower than the angels"? Is there any vantage point we can gain that will allow us to more appreciably perceive the distance the Visitor traversed? It's a tough problem: Where can I stand to gain even a glimpse of the distance between Deity and man?

All we do know in this present order of things is (1) man is lower than angels and (2) both are lower than God. But how from those propositions can I deduce the extent of His condescension? To attempt an answer, allow me to offer a thought without text, but which is wholly consistent with the spirit of God's Word, an imaginary trip which might help toward some notion of the degree of Christ's "being made lower" to visit us.

An excursion into eternity. Begin, please, by supposing yourself to have already been resurrected into the presence of the Lord. Jesus Christ has come for His Church, and she has already celebrated reunion with her Lord—the great wedding feast has already occurred. And, in this excursion into the realm of timelessness, ages upon ages have already rolled by when, one day, there comes a moment. . . .

The Lord Jesus Himself calls for you to come to Him at His throne. You appear in His presence, and with joy bow before Him inquiring of His will. He responds by inviting you to join Him on a journey.

"Where are we going, Lord?" you ask.

He replies, "To a place . . . a place in Father's universe. Come."

Suddenly, having traveled with your Lord at the speed of thought, you find yourself standing somewhere in the midst of the enormity of space, looking down on a small planet. He stands beside you, silently observing the orb, and then slowly extends His hand and points to it.

"This is the place of which I spoke," He says, "the place where I wanted to bring you."

"And for what purpose, my Lord?"

"Because I wish to talk with you about the creatures who dwell there. And from here you can see the place of their habitation."

You look from His face to the small world below. Distance prohibits any sign or notion of the beings who inhabit it.

The Lord continues. "It is important for you to understand what has transpired there before I ask a question of you."

"What question, my Lord?"

"I want to ask you your feelings about what action might be taken."

You look at the Lord of Glory with curiosity, and He explains. "The creatures of that world are creatures that you and I knew, on the world where we once lived, as 'dogs.'" He pauses pensively, then adds, "Father made them, you know."

Again you look down upon that speck in space, reminded somehow by the gentleness in the Savior's voice that the Infinite Power behind the creation of all things is also the

Infinite Lover of all that He has created.

As He continues speaking of the animals on the planet below, the Master observes, "Of course, I know that mankind has sometimes affectionately considered dogs 'almost human,' but they aren't. They are not even close to man in Father's order. For you," He says, turning to look deep into your eyes, "you are the only ones We have made in Our image."

The awareness of the uniqueness of man's destiny, and the high honor of his having been redeemed, moves you to worship—but the Lord is still speaking. "Dogs are of entirely another order; as different from man as fallen man was different from God." You nod with understanding, knowing now something of that dimensional difference since you have been in the eternal realm for ages long past.

"We are here," the Savior goes on, "because something very terrible has happened on that small planet. As it now stands, not one of these creatures remembers how they were first created. They neither understand how they were intended to live, nor recall their place in Father's created order—for Father creates nothing without purpose.

"Their tiny consciousnesses have been damaged. The understanding of purpose that Father and I engraved in every creature's awareness has been confused in these. They have become twisted within, and now they have all taken to deadly and vicious practices. Like the dogs you and I have seen on earth, they often travel in packs and. . . ." He pauses, sighing painfully. "And they fight with one another." He speaks haltingly, seeming to suffer their pain. "At times they rip and tear at each other. They seem to have lost

37

whatever they knew of their appointed design."

As He continues, the Great Shepherd of the universe seems to groan. "With this as it is, there's nothing they can do for themselves. They have no way to become again what Father meant for them to be at their beginning."

The look on His face stirs your compassion. You feel a heightened sensitivity to the Father's loving desire that all His creation—from stars and sons to donkeys and dogs— enjoy what He intended for their distinct purpose and fulfill-ment.

Then Jesus says: "I've brought you here to see this. And to ask you if . . . if you would consider going to them and explaining that they were created for something far better; to tell them that when the order of any part of Father's cre-ation is distorted, it grieves Him. Would you help Us show them Father's love in a way they can understand? If that were done, they might return to their intended order and stop their hateful and deadly ways."

He pauses, looking at you quietly, then asks, "Would you go to them for Us?"

Your heart feels the pulse of the divine love which has redeemed you, and you answer with a hesitant but honest question, "I want to do Your will, O Lord, but how shall I go?"

The Lord Jesus replies: "That's the most difficult part in My asking you, you see, because they will not be able to un-derstand anything other than a dog."

A dog? The full, crushing implications of His request de-scend upon you. For it is a request, not a mandate. Then He turns to face you and says: "You also need to know this. If you go, some of them will come to understand. The goal of their created purpose will be restored. But only some; not all of them will respond favorably."

A pause.

"As I told you, they have become wild. And some of them, in their wildness and viciousness, will turn on you, and. . . ." He seems reluctant to finish, but after a moment He goes on, "And they will kill you."

You turn to look toward a lost race of brute creatures, a breed of animals on a lonely planet in a darkened corner of the universe. Then, slowly, your eyes return to His. He speaks again.

"If you choose to go, I make you this promise. Your living and dying there will not be the end. But I will bring you back to be with Me to enjoy the delights of the glory—in Our presence. But for just a season, in order that those damaged creatures may understand Father's intended order for them, will you go?"

And it is here that we conclude our imagined scenario. Its purpose has been to say this, dear friend:

I have a great deal of love for human beings, and even a great deal of compassion for a wounded animal. But it is extremely difficult for me to imagine myself, for however noble a reason, stooping to the animal kingdom to become a dog. Something of the weight of what God did presses upon my soul as I measure the difference of the essential being between beasts and humans. How can the space between these two created orders be gauged? I can hardly imagine being asked to span such a gap by allowing the essential nature of my being to be altered to such a degree as to make possible my existence on an equal plane with a dog.

But I also hasten to affirm that the span between different created orders—between the human and animal kingdoms—is infinitely smaller than the span between the order of the Creator and His own creatures.

And yet, there was a day long ago when the Father said, "Son, You know that some will hear the truth and walk in Our way. But if You go, some of them will turn on You and . . . they will kill You. Will You go?"

In the light of this truth—that Christ consented to be made lower than the angels and suffer death—I invite you to "see Jesus." And in looking at Him, consider the richness of the great salvation He brought us—reaching so far, because He loves so much. What high destiny He sees in man, and it's one we only begin to apprehend when we grasp, at least in part, the degree of His condescension!

Let your soul praise Him!

> O marvelous and mighty Father God, thank You for visiting me. Thank You for sending Jesus, Your Son. Dear Jesus, thank You for condescending to become one of us. Thank You for coming to touch . . . to teach . . . to save. Holy Spirit, enlarge my understanding of the scope of Jesus' salvation—His coming, His suffering, His wounds, His blood, and His death—that I may see beyond tears to perceive the dynamic and the life You convey to me by those means. In Jesus' name, Amen.

PART TWO

HIS SUFFERING

Jesus Christ is risen today . . . Who did once upon the Cross suffer to redeem our loss. (Fifteenth-century hymn)

> Pain and affliction bearing,
> Frail is the flesh we're wearing.
> Mankind this weakness sharing,
>   Crying to be whole.
> Christ wore the stripes in sorrow,
> Paid all that we might borrow
> Health for a bright tomorrow,
>   Body, mind, and soul.
>
> J. W. H.

For it was fitting for Him, for whom are all things and by whom are all things, in bringing many sons to glory, to make the author of their salvation perfect through sufferings.

Therefore, in all things He had to be made like His brethren, that He might be a merciful and faithful High Priest in things pertaining to God, to make propitiation for the sins of the people. For in that He Himself has suffered, being tempted, He is able to aid those who are tempted. (Hebrews 2:10, 17, 18)

Who, in the days of His flesh, when He had offered up prayers and supplications, with vehement cries and tears to Him who was able to save Him from death, and was heard because of His godly fear, though He was a Son, yet He learned obedience by the things which He suffered. And having been perfected, He became the author of eternal salvation to all who obey Him. (Hebrews 5:7-10)

FIVE
THE SUFFERINGS OF CHRIST

WHAT IF?

What if Jesus had lived in virtual obscurity all of His life? What if His real identity had remained absolutely hidden, until one day He suddenly announced, "I am God"?

And what if, over the next few weeks, He preached several memorable sermons and performed a series of remarkable miracles to verify His divinity to onlookers—then, without prior warning, declared, "I will die to save all mankind"?

And what if His words one day so inflamed the anger of a mob that they killed Him instantly, and He died a victim of violence—a death virtually without pain—struck down in fury?

What if there had been no years of bone-wearying itinerant ministry, no bewildering rejection, no embittered accusations, no mock trial, no jeering, no beatings, no crown of thorns?

No crucifixion.

No suffering.

None at all.

It might have happened that way, you know. After all, the type of lamb that was slain on the altar of the Old Testament—the perfect symbol of the coming Lamb of God—was slain with just one rapid slit of the throat. The Old Testament sacrifice of animals didn't require agony. Only death. There was, then, a ritual precedent for the substitutionary sacrifice of a dying lamb. But not necessarily for a suffering one.

Why then, did the prophecy of Isaiah call for a suffering Messiah, ensuring that, in coming as the Visitor, Jesus Christ would endure a lifetime of struggle, loneliness, stress, temptation, pain, and anguish? And why should the visit require Him to die a slow, torturous death of crucifixion, rather than one of instant, painless demise? The answer is that this Lamb is a means of *restoration* as well as redemption, and His sufferings were an essential part of that mission.

THE SUFFERING SAVIOR

Throughout the history of the Church, the sufferings of Christ have often been depicted in such a way as to suggest God is saying to us, "The reason I had My Son suffer so much is that I wanted you always to remember and to be saddened by what your sin did." This mood is portrayed in much of the medieval and contemporary religious art forms, and it dominates the climate of many ecclesiastical rituals: "You hurt God! And don't you ever forget it!"

Now, there is an understandable and appropriate sense of shame and regret that should come to our hearts when meditating on what our Lord endured for our salvation. But

God's objective in Christ's suffering was not to produce that emotion in us. The suffering of Christ has more to do with our release and restoration—indeed, our joy—than with any divinely intended summons to feel shame.

Hebrews 2:10 says that through Christ's sufferings there was a *perfecting*, that is, a completion of His Saviorhood. That tells us this: The Son of God submitted to a plan that would include a lifetime of the same kind of suffering that you and I experience. And this plan would have something to do with setting us free from the oppressive power of that suffering.

A Savior who understands. "This High Priest of ours understands our weaknesses" (Heb. 4:15, TLB).

We all need someone who understands our feelings, our vulnerability both to emotional and physical pain. We need someone who identifies with the utter weakness of our flesh, especially before the ferocious onslaught of fear, doubt, anger, and lust—temptations which tear at the heart and rip out hope. Into this need for understanding Jesus comes, above all else wanting us to know that He does understand. His suffering has made Him the ultimate source to whom we can turn for understanding.

Twice, Scripture refers to the fact that Christ has "authored" our salvation (Heb. 5:9; 12:2). Both references address the fact that the actions by which He "wrote" were not accomplished by one quick stroke of a pen. The message He authors is not only one of forgiveness and eternal life being provided through His death. Added to this is His outline of a broader scope of salvation accomplished through His suffering. He introduces practical and powerful answers to life's tough times, bringing relief to the pressure points of our suffering.

It's as though Scripture is saying, "The Savior not only saves you from sin, but He understands you as a person. He has come to provide the way through and out of your suffering, just as surely as He has provided a way for your release from sin and its power. Come to Jesus, the author of eternal salvation. Since He 'wrote the book,' He understands every dimension and nuance of pain and suffering, and has an answer to it all."

His "authoring" of a complete salvation—through death and suffering—is a dual truth, profoundly described in the two passages in Hebrews that reveal Him as "author" in two different ways. In the first (5:9), the word *aitios* emphasizes His *causing* a complete salvation to be available to us. In the second (12:2), the word *archegos* underscores His *captaining* role—He leads us to full freedom through faith. He is both launcher and leader—He births a program of deliverance by His suffering, and He brings us through as He shares with us in our suffering.

But these facts do not solve the psychological dilemma most of us confront. The intellect probes while the emotions inquire—"How can He understand my suffering or really know what I feel?"

The first step in finding the answer to this is to avoid the mistake of confining Christ's sufferings to the Cross.

Through it all. We cannot diminish the reality of the fact that the Cross involved deep and agonizing suffering. From

the whipping post to the climax on Calvary, the record of
Christ's death is one of horrible pain:

His beard was torn from His face.

A crown of thorns was shoved into His head.

Nails were pounded into His feet and hands.

A spear split His side.

And in all of this, He refused to accept the sedative commonly given to those being crucified, choosing rather to tax
pain to its limit. But no amount of suffering could destroy
Him—not even suffering that resulted in death.

Yet, as real as the pain and agony at Golgotha were, there
is much more to understand about Christ's suffering for us
. . . and with us. To understand how thoroughly His triumph extends into the details of our human experiences of
stress and pain, we must look at more than Jesus' suffering
and death. We must look at His life.

Jesus understands hunger.

See Him in the wilderness after forty days of fasting, at
the point when the human body begins to consume itself
because it has used its own stored resources. That man being urged to create loaves from stones to satisfy Himself and
refusing to do so—that man understands hunger.

And He understands thirst.

The cry He makes from the Cross comes from parched
lips, dehydrated by extensive physical trauma. His "I thirst"
is more than the appeal of a day laborer coming in from a
scorching sun. This Man had been burnt dry by the hate of
cursing mockers, the fires of divine judgment, and the drain
of blood sacrifice. Jesus understands thirst!

Jesus also understands weariness.

As a small ship crosses Galilee, and a storm's fury terrifies His companions, Jesus sleeps. Strong men of experience who know the lake's many moods scream for help against the tempest's terror, yet the Visitor continues to sleep. His is not the sleep of the slothful or the lazy, nor of one insensitive to the crisis at hand. His sleep, undisturbed by the buffeting and roar of the storm, is indicative of a man who is completely depleted by fatigue. His physical frame is worn and His stamina spent from ministering to multitudes; so worn and weary is He that even the splashing of the waves, the whipping of the boat, and the shrieking of the wind cannot awaken Him.

If you ever feel so tired you can't take another step, and if you wonder whether God knows that feeling, here's your answer: There is One who not only knows your weariness, but who says, "I'll walk the next step with you because I've been where you are . . . and further."

But there's more than physical stress to life's sufferings. Consider the pain of being misunderstood. Of being rejected, mocked, or unjustly accused.

Consider the pain of being forgotten, of having people say you are evil for doing what you meant for good. Consider the pain of being unappreciated.

All of these pains are inflicted upon each of us . . . they are common to everyone.

Some may bite their lip, tighten their grip, and stoically insist, "It's all right; I can take it." But no one really can.

Not alone.

These things take an eventual toll on human nature. Un-

aided or untreated, the accumulation of such pain can provoke dour self-pity or produce an arthritis of the soul.
Sincere though our efforts at endurance may be, we can
become whiners on the one hand or brittle on the other.
Bracing ourselves against emotional pain without learning
to receive the support of the only One who has mastered it
by experience can only produce bitter fruit.

While saying, "It's all right," when it's really not, I can
turn into something monstrous. And it won't be "all right"
until I'm infused with the spirit of the One who truly knows
what it is to be rejected, to be unrewarded, to have impossi-
ble demands imposed . . . to be surrounded by nit-picking
critics who scrutinize every word and action, hoping for a
chance to find fault.

The suffering Savior knows all this: He's been through it
all. And He also knows man's inclination to feel God doesn't
really understand.

GOD LEADS A PRETTY SHELTERED LIFE

At the end of time, billions of people were scattered on
a great plain before God's throne. Some of the groups
near the front talked heatedly—not with cringing
shame before God's throne, but with embittered bel-
ligerence.

"How can God judge us? How can He know about
suffering?" snapped a brunette, jerking back a sleeve
to reveal a tattooed number from a Nazi concentration
camp. "We endured terror, beatings, torture, and
death!"

49

In another group, a black man lowered his collar. "What about this?" he demanded, showing the rope burns. "Lynched for no crime but being black! We've suffocated in slave ships, been wrenched from loved ones, and toiled 'til only death gave release."

Hundreds of such groups were visible across the plain. Each had a complaint against God for the evil and suffering He permitted in His world. How lucky God was, they all seemed to agree, able to live in heaven where all is sweetness and light; without weeping, fear, hunger or hatred. Indeed, what does God know about man? What does He know about being forced to endure the trials of life? After all, God leads a pretty sheltered life.

So each group sent out a leader, chosen because he had suffered the most. There was a Jew, a black, an untouchable from India, a person who was illegitimate, a person from Hiroshima, a Gulag veteran . . . and others who had tasted life's bitterest dregs. At last they were ready to present their case. It was rather simple: Before God would be qualified to be their judge, He must endure what they had endured.

Their decision was that God should be sentenced to live on earth as a man. But because He was God, they set certain safeguards to be sure He would not use His divine powers to help himself.

Let Him be a Jew.

Let the legitimacy of His birth be questioned.

Let Him champion a cause so just, but so radical, it

brings upon Him the hate, condemnation, and destructive attacks of political and religious authorities.

Let Him be betrayed and forsaken by His dearest friends.

Let Him be indicted on false charges, tried before a prejudiced jury, and convicted by a cowardly judge.

Let Him see what it is to be terribly alone and completely abandoned by every living being.

Let Him be tortured and . . . let Him die.

And let His death be humiliating; let it take place beside common criminals, while He is jeered at, mocked, and spit on.

As each leader announced his portion of the sentence, loud murmurs of approval went up from the great throng of people. But suddenly, after the last one had finished pronouncing sentence, there was a long silence. No one uttered another word. No one moved. For suddenly, all recognized the stark reality:

God had already served His sentence.

(Author unknown)

The Visitor understands suffering, and by reason of that understanding is not only fully accessible to our cry but fully able to give us release from the vicious power of suffering. He has absorbed it all in Himself, and He now stands ready to dispense relief and recovery with His word of peace amidst your torment.

Heartache and mental anguish
Rip at the soul, men languish.
Hellish the sword now brandished,
    Piercing human minds.
Comes now the Lord of healing,
Touched with our deepest feeling.
Truth from His lips is pealing,
    Freeing humankind.

J. W. H.

SIX
BUT COULD HE BE TEMPTED?

What does the Bible mean when it says Christ "suffered" temptation? I mean, after all, how can the quintessence of innocence and purity really be tempted?

But innocence means neither immunity nor invulnerability to sin; and purity means neither insensibility to nor incapability of sin. The mystery of the Incarnation, in which the divine and the human are fused into one, has caused many to wrestle with the question: "*Could* Jesus have sinned?"

This is a moot question now, because He didn't sin. Still, while it seems that His divine nature was not attracted by sin's power, His true humanity held the capability of sensing sin and needing to choose a response to it. Christ's absolute sinlessness would not have weakened the force and pain of temptation, it would have intensified it.

A person from outside who walks into a coal mine while wearing a white linen suit is obviously more vulnerable and sensitive to the dusty environment than those who are already blackened by their toil there. So it was with Jesus when He plunged into the mine shaft of this world's sin. Though sinless in Himself, He "suffered" the presence of sin around Him. In the midst of this—the painful pressure of the evil set against Him, taunting Him and saying, "Act now! Do anything You want!"—Christ *suffered* temptation.

Yet, the even greater reality of Jesus' victory over sin's pressure and temptation is that while clothed in perfect purity and walking through the inky mine of all that provokes and produces human sinning, Christ continually embraces the sinful. He regularly draws them to Himself and, amazingly, leaves each one imprinted with His holiness while He remains untarnished by sin's stain or power.

No, innocence is not immunity.

Preparing for a recent trip to Africa, the law required that I be vaccinated against several diseases common to the area of my intended visit. As with all such injections, I was given a vaccine containing the very viruses to which I would be vulnerable. Germs were literally put into my arm; some cholera, some typhoid—a small colony of each. Thus immunized, my body was able to form a resistance against the full force of these potentially fatal diseases.

But Jesus was not immunized against sin. He was not inoculated with "just a little" to brace His pure system against the shock of the world's sin and evil. Instead, because there was no sin in Him, His vulnerability to it and all of its ravages was so much the greater.

Since none of mankind has experienced sinlessness, we cannot understand the full force of Christ's suffering in sin's presence. We may be repulsed by sin on the grotesque or gross level, but the sting of sin's slightest presence is below our threshold of pain. We need to seek an understanding of Jesus' suffering of this sting.

We miss the mark if we make the mistake of supposing that His sinless life was a "no contest" match, making Him invulnerable to His opponent or somehow desensitized to sin's clawing efforts at entry into His pure nature. Jesus was tempted by the burning pressure of sin as it pressed on in its infectious quest to poison this Visitor from another realm. The fact that He was "tempted in all points like as we are, yet without sin," constitutes a dimension of suffering far beyond our comprehension. The presence and power of sin was been felt far more by this untarnished Visitor—this One who was new to the pollution of Earth's sooted, mine-like atmosphere—than we can ever grasp.

THE SUFFERER'S SAVIOR

There is yet another dimension of Christ's suffering that we would do well to study more carefully: "[He] suffered *for* us" (1 Pet. 4:1). Just as Christ's dying has accomplished a dual provision for us, so has His suffering. Every aspect of His redemptive work is rich with wealth for our resource.

Most of us readily understand how Jesus, in dying, paid the price of our sin and provided the gifts of life and forgiveness. But few realize that His suffering was more than merely a preliminary to His death: His suffering was redemptive, too! And His suffering was substitutionary. He suffered in our stead, absorbing in Himself the horrible implications of sin's impact on the human frame.

The Rotherham translation, though clumsy in its technical rendition of the Hebrew text of Isaiah 53:4, 5, nonetheless conveys the biblical truth with power:

"Yet surely our sicknesses he carried, and as for our pains he bare the burden of them. But we accounted him stricken, smitten of God and humbled. Yet was he pierced for transgressions that were ours, was crushed for iniquities that were ours. The chastisement for our well-being was upon him, and by his stripes there is healing for us."

The fact and the force. Jesus' suffering holds a provision for our healing. The preceeding passage from Isaiah, joined to Matthew 8:17 and 1 Peter 2:24, shows how completely biblical it is to reach out to the Lord Jesus Christ for deliverance from suffering and sickness. We can do this as surely as we can reach to Him for salvation from our sins.

Paul reminded early believers that their forgetfulness of the provisions of the Cross were even causing some to experience a premature death (1 Cor. 11:24-30). We should not fear hearing the Holy Spirit's voice speaking to us through the Word of God: "Forget not all His benefits: who forgives all your iniquities, who heals all your diseases" (Ps. 103:2, 3).

There is no question about the dimension of His promise. But there have been real questions at times with my own faith. Perhaps you, like I, find it easier to believe and receive forgiveness for my sins than to believe and receive healing for my body. Why that should be the case is beyond me, for it is clear that the greater miracle is the former: sin is a much greater problem than sickness!

It is marvelously joyous and precious to testify to the times we call upon the Lord for healing and experience it. But what about the times when faith seems weak, when healing seems remote—not because God is taunting or loveless, but because "healing faith" seems to elude us? At such a point, we tend to resign to either philosophy or bitterness; to rationalize the situation as "God's will" or to become angry, saying He doesn't care. But Christ, in going all the way through His sufferings, has provided a better alternative.

There is a force—a power—in Jesus' suffering to break the ability of pain, injury, or sorrow to dominate you, even when these things seem to persist beyond prayer. "For since he himself has now been through suffering . . . when we suffer . . . he is wonderfully able to help us" (Heb. 2:18, TLB). Christ's suffering has a power to absorb the most hellish or human attack, the most tragic or traumatic pain, or whatever it is that seems about to exceed your capacity to endure.

Without Christ, suffering can grind people down until they're reduced to emotional pulp, forced to surrender or driven to nervous exhaustion or breakdown. Suffering can so debilitate resistance that one finally concedes to sin— not because of lust, unbelief, or rebellion, but simply because of weariness in battle. But the transforming, revitalizing truth is that in His suffering, the Savior has penetrated the eye of the storm: He has shattered the power of suffering to destroy us.

Jesus has broken the ability of suffering to reduce us to bitterness, faithlessness, or disobedience. Hear Jesus whisper, "I want to fill you with the same life that brought Me through suffering; that kept Me from shrinking before the fires of hell's worst workings; that kept Me from wearying in well doing and from becoming bitter or turning to animosity. When I was unthanked, I didn't retaliate. When people rejected Me, I didn't withdraw My availability to love and serve them."

His life power is yours. Take it! Receive that part of your salvation that was purchased by His suffering for us! First, hear the Savior say, "Come to Me, I understand." Then hear Him add: "I will penetrate your suffering with My life, and not only will you survive but you will be victorious in the midst of it all!"

The Savior's sufferers. Before we conclude, one more facet of truth extends our meditation on Jesus' suffering for us. It is His call for people who will suffer *with* Him.

This may seem a peculiar focus, since our primary point has been His provision for deliverance from and victory through suffering. But we will miss a treasured truth if we overlook God's purpose for each of us in the suffering we have experienced. Even as He, having suffered, understands us, so He longs to minister to others through His people who have shared in His victory in the midst of their own pain. Just as the free gift of salvation is ministered to mankind by those who have received forgiveness and life in Christ, so the joy of victory over the power of suffering is given to others by those of us who have experienced His sustaining power: "That we may be able to comfort those who are in any trouble, with the comfort with which we ourselves are comforted by God" (2 Cor. 1:4).

Jesus is looking for people who will minister His life, His truth, and His love to other sufferers in the same spirit that He ministers to us. He is always patient with the suffering. He comes offering full healing and complete deliverance, but somehow many of His own are unable to receive everything He is willing to give. Weakness, fear, pride, spiritual blindness, doubt, or ignorance of the Word all have something to do with this. And yet, the perfect Savior who suffered for us is perfectly patient with me when I fail to grasp all He has for me.

And He calls us to be that way with one another. He points the way for us to partner with others in their suffering in the same way He has met us: with understanding and grace, and without criticism. In the Savior's call for "sufferers" to minister to the suffering, light is shed for us on some otherwise misunderstood passages in the Bible.

Romans 8:16, 17: "The Spirit Himself bears witness with our spirit that we are children of God, and if children, then heirs—heirs of God and joint heirs with Christ. . . ." We love that part! But it adds: "if indeed we suffer with Him, that we may also be glorified together."

Philippians 1:29: "For to you it has been granted on behalf of Christ, not only to believe in Him, but also to suffer for His sake."

Philippians 3:10: "That I may know Him . . . and the fellowship of His sufferings."

Many simply overlook or explain away such verses—still

others make them into a case for sickness and misery as a prerequisite to righteousness, as though God willed people to suffer. This train of thought can breed self-pitying, whimpering saints who lament: "God must want me to go through this suffering [sigh]. It's the cross He wants me to bear." But that isn't what these verses teach. To either deny or twist them in order to pretend that there are no suffering saints, or to strain them to frame a doctrine of "God-wills-my-suffering" is to miss the point on both sides.

SO SEND I YOU

In all of this Jesus is speaking to us, saying, "I have shown understanding of your suffering, and by My presence I have taught you that I can transform into victory the anguish, the pain, the burden, the pressure, and the inclination to give up. But, child, I offer you a partnership in an even greater victory—a triumph that exceeds any joy you've ever tasted."

And patiently He begins to teach us.

"Child, there are many you will touch who don't know the release, deliverance, and victory I have for them. These include My own, as well as others yet to enter the kingdom. I am asking you not to try to persuade them of truth, but to demonstrate its power in love. Suffer with them . . . patiently and with understanding.

"Their heads hang and their hearts droop with despair. They are overcome by burdens that are more than they know how to handle. They have not as yet learned the availability of My life-power in the midst of their suffering. Your words will not help them now—only your love.

"I have taught you of My presence and victory that you might answer this call. Will you go in My name and stand beside them? As I have come to you in your suffering, will you go now and suffer with them?

"Weep with those who weep.

"Be with those who are bound as though you also are bound.

"Lift up their feeble hands.

"Comfort their troubled minds.

"Bear one another's burdens and fulfill the law of Christ.

"As the Father sent Me to suffer and open the door to release . . . so send I you."

Loved one, have you ever sat with someone as they have spilled out the pain and hurt of disappointment, failure, or tragedy? Have you learned how they need much more than hurried, pretentious, all-knowing counsel? Job's comforters still plague the afflicted with their self-righteous attitude of "Now here's what you need to do about that!" But the parroting of Bible texts and theological truths is not their greatest need at the moment.

Oh, of course they need the Word! It will penetrate the deepest part of their being and bring comfort, hope, and correction. But the Word needs to be ministered sensitively, in the spirit of gentle counsel. The Word must be given as the incarnated Word—the Truth made flesh in you—revealed by your coming . . . your visiting . . . your loving. The best way for this to occur is when a sensible, sensitive soul comes beside the sufferer to say, "Listen, I understand.

I feel your pain and I'm going to stand with you through it. I don't have all the answers, but I am with you in the name of Him who does. But until we find His way through this, I'm here to suffer with you."

One of my most moving experiences was when a well-known man poured out to me the story of his moral failure and his dishonesty in business. It was painful for him, but he held nothing back. His contrition was real and his repentance deep.

When the conversation was nearly over, I turned to face Him squarely and said, "Brother, no matter what happens . . . no matter what is brought against you because of your failure, I make this commitment to you: I will stand by you on any terms, not only personally but also in public—not to affirm your guiltlessness, but to affirm my support to you as a brother in Christ."

I saw a strong and dynamic man reduced to tears. He took my hand as he said, "You've given me the greatest gift that anyone could possibly give me."

It is to such people that Jesus calls all of us. But we are not called just to know that He understands, that He has penetrated the core of the things that torment mankind and broken the power of suffering. He doesn't want us just to know that suffering can no longer reduce us to something less than God intends us to be. But now He says, "I want you to bring others to know these things as well! I want you to love them, realizing that loving them will often require you to suffer with them even as My loving you required that of Me."

It's a full circle, dear friend. Be healed in your suffering. Be released from your suffering. Both are provided in our salvation—His work "for us." Receive your wholeness, then go!

Go and be healing balm to a suffering world!

PART THREE

HIS WOUNDS

THERE HAS NOT FAILED ONE WORD
(Sing hallelujah)

There has not failed one word of all His promise.
All He has spoken He has done.
Stand on His Word, secure, unchang'd forever,
And Sing hallelujah!
Faithful God, our Father.

Whirlwinds of change are blowing cross the nations;
Storms of confusion blast and buffet all mankind.
Stands Christ our King, His "Peace, be still" commanding
And Now hallelujah!
I have peace unending.

With haunting doubt or passion of temptation
Satan would sift you or would seek to steal your joy.
Hear Jesus speak: "I've prayed for you, you'll fail not,"
And Sing hallelujah!
I am overcoming.

When in fiery furnace of affliction,
Hell's pow'r would cast you or some weakness lay you low.
Stand on His Word, "I am the Lord, your healer,"
And Sing hallelujah!
By His stripes He heals me.

Children of light, the darkness fast is gath'ring.
Earth's blackest midnight comes; its last travail begins.
Stand in the light; God's Word outshines the shadows,
And Sing hallelujah!
We've a bright tomorrow.

J. W. H.

SEVEN
THE WOUNDS OF CHRIST

For the law, having a shadow of the good things to come, and not the very image of the things, can never with these same sacrifices, which they offer continually year by year make those who approach perfect.

For then would they not have ceased to be offered? For the worshipers, once purged, would have had no more consciousness of sins. But in those sacrifices there is a reminder of sins every year. For it is not possible that the blood of bulls and goats could take away sins.

Therefore, when He came into the world, He said: "Sacrifice and offering You did not desire, But a body You have prepared for Me. In burnt offerings and sacrifices for sin You had no pleasure. Then I said, 'Behold, I have come—in the volume of the book it is written of Me—To do Your will, O God.'"

Previously saying, "Sacrifice and offering, burnt offerings, and offerings for sin You did not desire, nor had pleasure in them" (which are offered according to the law), then He said, "Behold, I have come to do Your will, O God." He takes away the first that He may establish the second. By that will we have been sanctified through the offering of the body of Jesus Christ once for all. (Hebrews 10:1-10)

It is too frequently the case that Christ's sufferings and His wounds are seen as one and the same. Yet each are specific expenditures within redemption's full purchasing price. Each feature of the Visitor's experience secures a potential for our triumph over the effects of specific issues in life that we could never overcome through our own efforts. That's what Hebrews 10:1 really means: The law (our own efforts) can never make those who approach God perfect. The following verses of the text explain why that is true.

FORETOLD BUT NOT FORESHADOWED

The Old Testament Scriptures foreshadowed many of the features of Christ's impending fulfillment of God's plan of salvation. One detail after another, through a "dim foretaste" or a "shadow," was shown forth.

For example, Jesus was foreshadowed as the Lamb of God: (1) slain before the foundation of the world and (2) sent to take away the sin of the world. In that "shadow," the sacrificial lamb of the Old Testament forecast the substitutionary death of Christ, the Lamb God gave to be the covering for our sins. In remarkable detail a silhouetted forecast of the coming Savior was shown in the Levitical system. But there was one thing that the Old Testament sacrificial lamb did not foreshadow: the wounded Christ.

When sacrificed according to Moses' directive, lambs were killed quickly. . . mercifully. . . in a moment. Not only was a lamb not wounded, but to qualify for sacrificial purposes each animal had to be bruise- and blemish-free. Interestingly enough, the very perfection that God required of a sacrificial animal—to foreshadow the perfect sacrifice He would eventually provide—disallowed a wounded creature being used for the Old Testament sacrifices. Yet while the wounds of Christ were not *foreshadowed* in that Old Testament type, they were *foretold* by the prophets.

The pathway of understanding begins with the quotation of Psalm 40 in our text: "Sacrifice and offering You did not desire; my ears You have opened; burnt offering and sin offering You did not require. Then I said, 'Behold I come; in the scroll of the Book it is written of Me. I delight to do Your will, O my God, and Your law is within my heart.'"

These words are taken from a passage which scholars agree predicted the coming of Messiah. But we are given history as well as prophecy, for we are expressly informed that when the Son of God left the glory world to enter this one, He spoke these words from Psalm 40—words written by David a thousand years earlier. In light of those facts, might we ask, "When did Jesus Christ actually 'say' these words?" The answer is only clear if we see the setting: an actual conversation between the Son—Second Person of the Trinity—and the Father—First Person of the Trinity, just as Jesus was preparing to leave the Father's throne to come to earth. Let your thoughts fly with mine to a scene in the eternal past; a scene which occurs in the very throne room of highest glory.

Only a few places in the Bible give a glimpse of heaven. Ezekiel describes his vision of God's glory and Isaiah describes his sense of being ushered before God's throne (Ezek. 1, 3; Isa. 6). Perhaps the most panoramic scene of the throne is drawn by John as he records his vision of the throng at worship in the Book of Revelation (chapters 4, 5). Those scenes project a throne room so enormous, so expansive that it has a virtual lake—a "crystal sea"—in front of God's throne. Here innumerable hosts worship, as praise echoes through the halls of this arenalike cathedral, the enormity of which staggers our imaginations.

The Bible hardly gives us a complete picture of the Godhead—the Trinity—enthroned. Who can imagine it? But what we do know is that the Son of God is seated on the right hand of the Father: He was there before all worlds, long before becoming flesh to dwell among us, always having been ever-present with the Father and the Spirit.

And can you imagine that here, in the splendor of this throne room, a moment occurred, one that the Bible speaks of as an instant in the timelessness of eternity. The Father, the Son, and the Holy Spirit took counsel together concerning the projected plan of man's creation; a plan requiring the provision of a Redeemer. It was here, on His own initiative, that the Son agreed to be that Redeemer—agreed that, when need dictated and the Father directed, He would go to mankind's rescue.

Now the decision has been inscribed in the annals of eternity. It will be much later that this will be announced by the prophet and written in the Father's Book on earth: "Unto us a Child is born . . . a Son . . . given." Thus, we gain a glimpse into why it is that the Bible says, "Before the foundation of the world: the Lamb of God was slain."

Let such a scene provoke thankful praise. Before time as we know it began, man's salvation was considered and planned in the counsel chambers of heaven!

But now, our imaginations moving out beyond that juncture in eternity, we step into time and begin to trek the centuries which tabulate the cavalcade of man's history. We reach a point in which time's passage has long been in progress. Creation, the Flood, Babel, and Abraham are far behind. We have moved past Israel's Egyptian bondage, their deliverance, and the passage of the Red Sea. The Ten Commandments have been given, the wilderness journey is behind, the Promised Land has been fought for and taken. Israel's and Judah's kings have come and gone, as has the Babylonian captivity and the return of the remnant from that exile.

We enter the silent period where prophetic voices seem stilled. A holy hush has enveloped the heavenlies, as all creation anticipates the coming fulfillment of generations of divinely inspired prophecy.

Then it happens.

The fullness of time has come and the Father is ready to send forth His Son. And it is precisely then that He turns to His Son, and on the basis of an agreement made ages ago, He simply says, "Now."

They gaze at one another momentarily, as both Father and Son knowingly weigh the moment and its cost. Then, without hesitation, in a gesture containing actions and implications beyond our grasp, the Son lays aside garments of glory and turns to the Father with these words. "You were not satisfied with the animal sacrifices, slain and burnt before You as offerings for sin. . . . See, I have come to do Your will, to lay down My life, just as the Scriptures said that I would" (see Heb. 10:6, 7).

From glory to a womb. Can we fathom all that really happened in that moment—in that miracle of miracles? Jesus' preincarnate glory was not in the kind of body we're used to seeing. We cannot imagine His form. This is not to suggest that He had some bizarre, extraterrestrial frame, but simply to assert, as the Epistle to the Philippians says, that He was then "in the form of God" (2:6). Yet He lays aside whatever that form expresses in its eternal splendor, and willingly takes on a human form—the physical expression of man, the creature: "It has been written in the volume of the Book and now I go, to take on that body You have readied for Me."

But at that moment, the "body" is hardly a body at all. It is but a cell in the womb of a virgin, in a small city of a tiny nation, in one small corner of a fallen planet.

In one microsecond, the primal form of the Son disappears from the throne room of heaven, and in that same split-moment, the Holy Spirit of God has placed the life of the Second Person of the Godhead within the womb of a maiden.

The inconceivable has been conceived.

The Word will become flesh.

God will live and breathe among us.

And in coming to take that body, He also knows full well

that, unlike the sacrificial lamb foreshadowing Him, He will be wounded. The Book which said, "A body will be prepared," has also written into it additional provisional clauses: Salvation will require that the sacrifice be indelibly wounded with marks that will tell eternally of the fact a divine visit was made. And in His coming, He is consenting to every word . . . "to do Your will, O God" (Heb. 10:7).

The prophecies say: "He was wounded for our transgressions, He was bruised for our iniquities" (Isa. 53:5). And He who is taking on this "prepared body" to fulfill those words knows what they mean: *wound* means broken flesh; *bruise* means a beaten body.

A body made for wounding. Jesus knew that the body He would take on earth would be wounded, bruised, beaten, battered, slapped, and have the face hairs pulled out. Isaiah had spoken of Him, "I give My back to those who struck Me, and My cheeks to those who plucked out the beard" (Isa. 50:6). He would also be beaten for our peace, the whippings leaving stripes that would be an agency for mankind's healing (Isa. 53:5). Other prophetic statements awaited confirmation by His coming for wounding:

> For dogs have surrounded Me; The assembly of the wicked has enclosed Me. They pierced My hands and My feet. (Psalm 22:16)
> And I will pour on the house of David and on the inhabitants of Jerusalem the Spirit of grace and supplication; then they will look on Me whom they have

pierced; they will mourn for Him as for his only son, and grieve for Him as one grieves for a firstborn. (Zechariah 12:10)

Climactically, Isaiah 52:14 puts it this way: "So His visage was marred more than any man." Franz Delitzsch, the renowned Old Testament and Hebrew language scholar, unfolds the force of the expression used in the Isaiah reference. He explains that the language here conveys a prophecy of a person being so distorted that all likeness to a man is destroyed. Complete disfigurement, until all that remains is a grotesque, battered hulk.

So it is that the fact of His wounding was only revealed through the words of the prophets, for no animal type *could* reveal it. Through prophetic lips and pens, the Holy Spirit declared that Jesus would come, not only as a bleeding, dying lamb, but as a suffering and wounded man. And when Christ said, just prior to His entry into our world, "See, I have come to do Your will, O God," He fully understood the implication of those words. He would be required to fulfill all the revealed, prophesied, written will of God.

And the Visitor came to bear those wounds.

EIGHT
WHY WAS HE WOUNDED?

The Bible gives distinct reasons for Christ's wounds, and explains how they apply to us: "By that will we have been sanctified through the offering of the body of Christ once for all" (Heb. 10:10). The Word specifically says that the wounded *body* of Christ is a specific part of God's means for sanctifying us, that is, in making our bodies His own, as well as our souls. Something about Jesus' wounds applies directly to us personally—in fact, to our very physical beings.

The practical relationship between Christ's wounds and our bodies becomes clear when we recall how sin has tainted our bodies. Of course, the issue of our sin has been settled through His blood; the heart can be assured of peace with God—all has been forgiven. But how often, even after the confidence of forgiveness of sin, do shame and the memory of those sins still lurk within us? The body we live in so often carries remembrance of sin in its very members; from thoughts our minds have entertained to paths our feet have walked. All of us, at some time, have given our bodies to actions unworthy of a creature made in God's image and intended to live in God's will.

75

God's gift of salvation through the Cross brought us a rich resource of forgiveness and new birth. But with this gift, God addresses us as more than saved souls. He speaks about our bodies, too: "Do you not know that your body is the temple of the Holy Spirit?" (1 Cor. 6:19).

Are you tempted to doubt that claim, to abjectly say, "My body, Father? Your words are too much for me. You can't mean this flesh which has been given to selfishness, sensuality, sinning, and disobedience! Perhaps it can be a dwelling for a forgiven child, but hardly a temple for Your Holy Spirit." Still, the Bible says our bodies are temples, and that God sent Jesus *in a human body*—that our human bodies might be sanctified unto God when Christ offered up His body!

Applying the truth. This is exactly where we need the work of the wounded Savior applied to our lives. There must come a point in our experience when we know not only the confidence of forgiveness of sins, but the certainty of bodies acceptable to God.

In His wounds, Christ provides a way of removing us from the guilt and shame of our past that still seem to be associated with, and thereby attached to, the parts of our bodies that were given to sin.

Jesus says, "Though your back was stiffened against God, I paid the price when I let them wound My back. I call you 'holy,' because the evidence against you is no more."

Jesus says, "Your face has twisted and sneered with impudence, scorn, criticism, and pride. But because My beard was ripped out and My face slapped—by those wounds I have removed all earlier claims to your countenance, and have set it apart as Mine. My glory on your face is justly yours to bear, and you need never say, 'Lord, how can I look at myself, or upon You?'"

Here is the crux of this truth: The wounds of Christ have direct points of application to those things that have happened to debase or demean our bodies. God's Word says that the blood of Christ literally includes the power to cleanse our bodies from stain and—even beyond that—to purge our consciences from the shameful memories related to those deeds (Heb. 9:13, 14). Further, Philippians 3:21 declares that at His coming, Christ "will transform our lowly body that it may be conformed to His glorious body." This text more directly refers to the ultimate physical translation our bodies will experience when Jesus comes again.

But hear this, dear one: Just as surely as there will be a future moment of physical glorification—a complete eternal change in our bodies—so it is that there is a limited but real present manifestation of His kingdom glory in and through us now. *That's* the message of our study: Jesus took a human body to fulfill a precise aspect of the Father's will. The wounds sustained in His body are to break the shame of past sins performed by our own bodies, blotting out the memories of sins that often cause us to feel disqualified as physical vessels to be used for His purpose. His physical wounds establish the Father's full possession and dominion in our bodies, as certainly as His forgiveness has done that in our souls.

According to the Word of God, this very moment you are sitting in a dwelling place that is fully qualified for heaven's purposes: your body! Your body has been sanctified, made worthy by God Himself to be a residence of His Holy Spirit, a temple for His indwelling. That physical frame you live in, whatever its past abuse or present weakness, is being raised by the Holy Spirit as a shrine unto the God of the heavens!

Pause a moment with me, and open your hands in front of you.

Look at them.

They are *your* hands. And God calls them "holy hands" (1 Tim. 2:8). He has qualified those hands to be instruments of worship. They answer to the divine prescription: "Who may climb the mountain of the Lord? . . . only those with pure hands and hearts" (Ps. 24:3, 4, TLB). It isn't hypocrisy to lift those hands before Him in praise, and it isn't dishonest to extend those hands in service, however marred they may be by past sinning. For now Jesus is saying, "Look to Me, child. I was wounded in that exact place. Therefore, before hell's taunts and in the face of your doubts, I declare that those hands are Mine. Your hands are worthy because My hands were pierced. They have been restored to Me by My wounds!"

But the fact that Christ's sanctifying wounds cover our hands is only the beginning. Our entire bodies—their deliverance and their dedication—are given grounds for a total release. Hear the Word: "And do not present your [physical] members as instruments of unrighteousness to sin, but present yourselves to God as being alive from the dead, and your members as instruments of righteousness to God" (Rom. 6:13). Jesus is saying: "You are not your own anymore. My feet and hands were pierced, My heart was stabbed through, My body was broken—and through this I've laid claim to all those parts of you by My wounds. You have been sanctified, set apart to My purpose."

And suddenly, it becomes clear that in saying "You are not your own," Jesus is doing more than declaring His rightful ownership. Since I have been bought with the price of His whole being, He is telling me that He has both freed all of me and established the full worthiness of every member of my body for His use. I am free to be His, separated unto Him by His wounds.

The shame of the past. Once while speaking in another city, the Holy Spirit gave me a word of knowledge: "There is a woman here," I said, "who has dressed as she always does, with a long-sleeved blouse that buttons around the wrist."

There were hundreds in the room; the description was not distinctive, but I continued, "You always wear that sleeve length for the explicit purpose of covering scars which remain from a suicide attempt you made some time back. Today I address you in Jesus' Name, and His word to you is that His wounds are sufficient to cover yours. You need no longer bear the shame of them nor fear seeing those wounds which have taunted you as though saying, 'You'll try to do it again.' Today Christ says instead, 'The shame is past and the future is secure. Receive My full provision for you.'"

When that service concluded, a young woman came forward. She unbuttoned and lifted her sleeves to display the scars she sought to hide from herself as well as others. She later explained how the imprints truly had seemed to speak to her—to argue that her inescapable, eventual destiny was suicide.

Her face was now a study in joy, radiant and washed with tears. She said, "I'm the woman you spoke of, and I'm showing you these scars for two reasons: I know I've been released from shame, and I know I don't need to be afraid of them anymore." And she was free.

Her story may resemble yours. What part of your body is being snatched at by the adversary? How is he seeking to drag you down? Have wrong attitudes found expression on your face—a jaw that juts arrogantly, an eye that leers, or a mouth that smirks? And what does your body language communicate? Do your shoulders droop indifferently, do you have a stance that sneers defiance, or do you walk with a macho swagger or seductive swing that seeks to appeal inappropriately?

How much of our lives, our security, and our identity are related to or declared by our physical demeanor and bearing? To this the Lord Jesus says, "My wounds were to gain ownership of that part of you. Not that I might dominate you oppressively, but that I might give you freedom through deliverance. I have been wounded so you can be whole." His wounds hold the keys to releasing our bodies from any power that traps them.

And thus God's Word appeals: "I beseech you therefore, brethren . . . present your bodies a living sacrifice, holy, acceptable to God" (Rom. 12:1). With His wounded body, Jesus has purchased the privilege of requesting from us the living sacrifice of dedicated lives and worshipful praise.

A SCARRED SAVIOR . . . FOREVER

There is a curious fact about Jesus' post-Resurrection appearances to His disciples. Although He was completely and miraculously healed of His wounds, the scars could still be seen. I say this seems "curious," because the body in which He appeared to them was a "glorified" body—that is, one that lives by spiritual energy instead of physical energy. It is the same body He will have forever, which clearly indicates that when we stand before Him in our eternal bodies—without wound, scar, or any deficiency—His body will remain marked by Calvary's wounds!

I have a scar on my wrist where I burned myself when I was just a boy. I have another scar on my abdomen from surgery I experienced years ago as an adult. These are but two of a half-dozen scars on my body, all of which will be absent when I receive an eternal body at the resurrection. But the Bible reveals that heaven will contain One who will bear scars throughout eternity: His name is Jesus, our Lord. And John records seeing Him beside the throne as a lamb with "the fresh marks of slaughter" still visible on His body. (See Phillips and New English Bible translations of Revelation 5:6.)

One might ask, "Does He *have* to bear them forever?" The answer isn't known, but the Bible does show them there in the scriptural photograph we are given of our ascended King.

In a previous chapter we took an imaginary journey into the timelessness of eternity to witness the Son's consent to visit us, and to see Him receive the body prepared for His earthly sojourn. Now, will you come there again, this time to witness His return from His earth-mission to the glory world and the Father's presence?

In preparation for this journey, look at Psalm 24, seeing it as part of the trilogy of prophetic psalms (Pss. 22-24): Psalm 22 depicts Jesus the Savior; Psalm 23 displays Jesus the Shepherd caring for His flock; Psalm 24 describes Jesus the Sovereign at His ascension. It is to the latter psalm that we turn to glimpse His return to heaven, his triumphant entry into glory to assume again His majestic throne.

The word *gates,* as used in this psalm, is the term for "authorities"—spiritual beings of power. So the command, "Lift up ye gates!" is not addressing doors to a heavenly citadel. Rather this is a summons, issued to the angelic host around the throne, to praise. Here's what the psalm says:

> Lift up your heads, O you gates! And be lifted up, you everlasting doors! And the King of glory shall come in. Who is this King of glory? The Lord strong and mighty, the Lord mighty in battle. Lift up your heads, O you gates! And lift them up, you everlasting doors! And the King of glory shall come in. Who is this King of glory? The Lord of hosts, He is the King of glory. (Psalm 24:7-10)

How many of the heavenly host were witness to the Son's earthly sojourn? Peter hints that they wanted to look in on what was being fulfilled in Christ, but they weren't allowed to know what was happening until after His ascension (see

1 Peter 1:12). Certain angels did announce Jesus' birth. Others ministered to Him following His temptation, and an angel helped sustain Him in Gethsemane (Luke 22:43). But it seems that, generally speaking, angels are absent during Christ's ministry—especially at Calvary. In spite of their availability to Him (Matt. 26:53), Jesus refuses to seek rescue or aid from heaven's hosts.

And so it is that, until He reappears in glory in heaven, the hosts have not conceived of the Son in his present form: a man scarred for eternity. They would have remembered Him in His resplendent eternal form when from eternity He was seated beside the Father in a form we can neither describe or imagine. Most had not seen Him since that moment when He suddenly was gone, going to reside in a womb as a human embryo, to one day become a man.

But now the Father summons the host to rise: "Lift up your heads, you gates! The King of glory is returning!" Can you picture the bewilderment on the angelic faces? Every head turns to welcome the Second Person of the Godhead back to His throne and there they see a man—a *wounded* man!

His return is as sudden as His departure; the hosts anticipate the joy of reunion with the Beloved One. But upon rising at the Eternal Father's command, their voices and instruments set for a welcoming fanfare, they are stunned; heaven's hosts themselves surprised! They hadn't expected Him to come as a man when He returned. Perhaps He would sojourn as one, but to be a man for an eternity? They had sacrificed heaven's dearest treasure in sending Him, and now the return on their investment is a glorious—but wounded—man! And as this man strides toward them, you can almost hear them ask, "Is this the Son . . . or is He not here yet?" But a crescendoing, assuring word rises from the throne.

"This is He, you hosts," declares the Almighty, "My beloved One. He is the Lord strong and mighty, the Lord mighty in battle. He has gone forth, fought victoriously, and returns scarred. Look up! Let us rejoice, for He is back. Lift up your heads, O you gates! Lift them up, you everlasting doors! And the King of glory shall come in."

The angels cast one last bewildered look at the approaching man and find that it *is* He—Lord Sabbaoth, the Lord of hosts! The King of glory! And the anthems of heaven begin to rise as the angels endlessly shout: "Worthy is the Lamb . . . Worthy is the Lamb!"

One poet has caught the heartbeat of this text and proposed this angelsong for the King's ascent:

> Lift up your heads eternal gates,
> Ye everlasting doors.
> The Son of God triumphant
> Is returning from the wars.
> Lift up your heads eternal gates,
> Loud let the anthems swell;
> The dynamite of Calvary
> Has smashed the gates of hell.

The Lamb who returns to glory bears wounds; but each one heals brokenness in human lives and declares the worth of human potential as God views it. He visits to bear wounds, for by His estimate the wounded are worth it. Unto Him be glory forever, for He is worthy.

Praise Him with me, will you? He is the Lamb, wounded for us that we might be whole both now and forever.

PART FOUR
HIS BLOOD

Now when these things had been thus prepared, the priests always went into the first part of the tabernacle, performing the services. But into the second part the high priest went alone once a year, not without blood, which he offered for himself and for the people's sins committed in ignorance; the Holy Spirit indicating this, that the way into the Holiest of All was not yet made manifest while the first tabernacle was still standing.

It was symbolic for the present time in which both gifts and sacrifices are offered which cannot make him who performed the service perfect in regard to the conscience—concerned only with foods and drinks, various washings, and fleshly ordinances imposed until the time of reformation.

But Christ came as High Priest of the good things to come, with the greater and more perfect tabernacle not made with hands, that is, not of this creation. Not with the blood of goats and calves, but with His own blood He entered the Most Holy Place once for all, having obtained eternal redemption. For if the blood of bulls and goats and the ashes of a heifer, sprinkling the unclean, sanctifies for the purifying of the flesh, how much more shall the blood of Christ, who through the eternal Spirit offered Himself without spot to God, purge your conscience from dead works to serve the living God?

And for this reason He is the Mediator of the new covenant, by means of death, for the redemption of the transgressions under the first covenant, that those who are called may receive the promise of the eternal inheritance. (Hebrews 9:6-15)

NINE
THE BLOOD OF CHRIST

It has often been told that chemists search for the universal solvent; a solution which can remove all stains and dissolve all bonds. Yet should they find it they would be incapable of producing a dispenser, for it too would dissolve.

But there *is* such a solvent. Only one. And the dispenser was the human body of God's only Son.

It is common in the writings of most hymn writers, poets, and theological authors to capitalize the word *blood* when referring to the blood of Jesus. They are well aware it is a substance of tremendous significance. In the blood of Christ, we touch the heart of God's redemptive plan.

There is an awesome responsibility on the part of believers to understand the importance of blood. The fact that almost everyone is emotionally affected by the sight or thought of blood is of no small significance. We shudder to think of taking a life, and there is a deep-seated reaction with regard to bloodshed. We sense its essential part in our physical survival and often are revulsed simply by the sight of blood.

Then God becomes involved and, although some want to dismiss it from thought, He becomes very serious about a program of rescue that demands blood. God deals with the matter head on: "Without shedding of blood there is no remission" (Heb. 9:22). Why? Our human sensitivities cry for an answer.

Fourteen hundred years before Christ—3,400 years ago—the Lord spoke, saying:

> The life of the flesh is in the blood, and I have given it to you upon the altar to make atonement for your souls; for it is the blood that makes atonement for the soul. (Leviticus 17:11)

In these words, God explicitly says that the atonement for man's sin, the reconciliation, was at the price of blood, and that He was *giving* that payment to man. But He also makes a categorical statement about man's life: "The life of the flesh is in the blood." That fact was penned by Moses circa 1440 B.C. Since then, the physiological truth of that scriptural statement has been proven time and again.

The function and survival of the human body depend on blood; indeed, the body's essence is wrapped up in it. And although science has only lately verified that fact, over three millenia ago God was seeking to draw man's attention to the blood's significance: "Your life, O Man, is totally dependant upon blood." And it is *that* substance, the essence of our existence, that forms the foundation for securing the salvation of the human race.

Thus, God breathed the breath of life into Adam . . . and every living creature enjoys life in that same way. Once birth has occurred, breathing must begin, for life comes to us one breath at a time! And when it comes it is rushed to every cell by the blood that courses through the veins. Yet, oddly enough, that river which carries life stops when its precious cargo—oxygen—is stopped. So it should come as no surprise that blood is at the heart of redemption's program, for it is the very center of life!

And at the heart of it all, God found it necessary for Himself, the Creator, to partake "of flesh and blood" (Heb. 2:14). He knew He had to show us how to live life in its fullest, and to pour Himself out as a sacrifice for our death-deserving twistedness.

In the future. The theme of the blood of Christ will occupy the endless ages of eternity. Referring to the redeemed as they gather around the throne of God, the Bible says, "And they sang a new song saying, 'You are worthy to take the scroll, and to open its seals; for You were slain and have redeemed us to God by Your blood out of every tribe and tongue and people and nation, and have made us kings and priests to our God'" (Rev. 5:9, 10).

It is clear in this passage that voluntary praise for the blood of Christ will fill eternity. Knowing what we do of God's ways and nature, we can safely conclude that the eternal song will continue for a definite reason: God did not bring us to that point to be chanting robots, but we will forever be gaining insight into the wisdom of God's way of restoration through the blood of the Lamb. Now, if the passing aeons will increase our gratitude, how wise we would be to consider how much our present life can be enhanced by prayerful, thoughtful meditation on the blood of Jesus.

As you can see, this is no casual theme. We are at the very heart of all physical life and at the core of all human salvation. Little wonder then that it is the basis of eternal praise!

The blood speaks. Here is something of a mystery about blood: It speaks. We are first introduced to this phenomenon in reading the fourth chapter of Genesis.

Cain has killed Abel, his brother, and the Lord has come to challenge him on the issue of the murder.

"Where is Abel, your brother?" God inquires.

Cain answers, "How should I know? Am I supposed to keep track of him wherever he goes?"

And then the Lord makes this telling statement: "The voice of your brother's blood cries out to Me from the ground" (Gen. 4:9, 10). With these words we are given this revelation: blood transcends the physical realm in its influence and significance.

Further evidence of the supra-physical qualities of blood is seen in God's instructions to the Israelites. Among the ordinances given when they prepared to occupy Canaan was the Lord's direction that if a body was found slain in an open field, and the murderer be untraced, a sacrifice must be offered by residents of the nearest city. Otherwise, the defilement of guilt for the blood that was violently shed there fell on the people of that community. Such was the power of the presence and witness of blood (Deut. 21:1-9). In a similar context, God spoke concerning the sin, bloodshed, and violence of Sodom and Gomorrah: "I am going down to see whether these reports are true or not. Then I will know" (Gen. 18:21, TLB). Bloodshed bears a testimony of its own.

The force of this concept comes to bear on us with reference to the blood of the Cross. In Hebrews 12:24, we are told to consider, since the blood of Abel bore a testimony, how much more the blood of Christ "speaks better things" for us.

The point is clear.

Just as Abel's blood cried for God's justice where injustice had been committed, Jesus' blood also cries out for God's action. But, His blood is not calling for justice to be done, rather it is declaring that justice has been accomplished. It is because of that power of blood to bear witness that Jesus' first words from Calvary, spoken as the first blood is shed, are "Father, forgive them." And the message He sounded forth then continues to work forgiveness now. This fact is underscored in our text. The present tense verb form of *speaks* emphasizes the present ongoing action: Jesus' blood is still speaking.

There is a continuous testimony still being borne to the excellence in the power of and effectiveness for cleansing by the blood that was spilled on a Judean hillside centuries ago.

With the theme of the blood, we enter enormous dimensions of truth. There is a splendor here—something beautiful, glorious, and unfathomable in the blood of Christ. It is not a morbid study, but a positive, powerful, and dynamic one. God's Word unveils the meaning of the blood of Christ from three perspectives: as a *tradition,* a *transaction,* and a *transfusion.*

THE TRADITION OF THE BLOOD

In Hebrews 9, the sacrifices offered by the Old Testament priests are shown to be symbolic; although the opening words note that the Old Testament ordinances concerning blood sacrifice had specific ritual patterns that needed to be literally observed. In their symbolism, these ordinances were somewhat like a painting. It was God's way, through traditional observances, to introduce His people to what He was preparing for them in the future. It is important for us to understand that these laws and ordinances were not an end in themselves. David understood that long before the coming of Christ (Ps. 51:16, 17)! The New Testament teaches us that the Old Testament ordinances were given as a schoolmaster—a tutor to help bring us to Christ in the same way that a child is trained until he can come into his own full potential (see Gal. 3:24).

The law of the sacrifices was the schoolroom for mankind, intending to bring him to God's highest and best. As with any early schooling, the goal is not the student's recitation of the alphabet, but his learning to arrange those letters into words and read them with understanding; he isn't expected just to learn the multiplication tables, but he is taught so that he may gain the ability to solve mathematical problems. And so it was with the Old Testament traditions: God was, in essence, teaching ABC's and multiplication tables so that, by these lessons, man would later be able to understand His plan and purpose in the Redeemer He would send and in the redemption He was to provide.

Against the backdrop of the legal traditions of the law of Moses, life and death can be discerned. From the ABC's of tradition, we can discover the One who is the Word. And in reading of Him, we learn the mathematics of life's meaning: He is the sum of all and the focus of the letters of the Law. Everything adds up in Him, and life's purposes multiply when we learn to solve our problems through Christ.

So the traditions and symbols had a purpose. In the midst of them all, God was teaching preliminary lessons for the more advanced teachings mankind would need to learn.

Sin is serious. The first lesson mankind could discern through the traditions of the Law was that sin cannot go unremitted, unpaid for. Payment must be exacted for all sins committed.

The world's mindset observes sin casually, as a sort of sorry trait of the race, and the less said about it the better. "You know how things are," someone says with a shrug. "It's too bad . . . just let it go." Most of us agree that it's unfortunate that people are thoughtless and unkind, that tempers fly and violent events occur, that trust is violated and integrity compromised. "But what can you do? It's human nature." And with that, as though sin were a mere whimsy, the issue of sin, its root, and its fruit, is philosophically dispensed with. The world emits a sigh of hopeless indifference as its deepest sign of regret.

This spirit must be confronted or it will too readily dilute our understanding. True human freedom will never evolve from rationalizing our sin, and this casual view must be identified and uprooted wherever it may have seeped into the mindset of believers.

But many who receive Christ carry into their new life the empty theology of their surrounding culture. And unless this vacuum of "pop theology" is filled with truth, empty ideas will produce barren hearts which lead to hollow living.

How does the Bible view sin?

The Bible teaches that sin is more than a "religious issue." It touches all of man's existence, disjointing and warping his world. It poisons and pollutes and stains wherever it flows—a people, their society's fabric, or an entire economic order. Sin results in death. It is an ultimate issue because it ultimately issues in ruin—the ruination of everyone and everything.

Something must be done about sin. It cannot be swept under a carpet; it has to be dealt with. God says so: "The wages of sin is death. . . . All the rest of the world around us is under Satan's power and control, . . . doomed forever for [their] sins . . . lost, without God, without hope. . . . You will perish unless you leave your evil ways. . . . Why will you die?" (Rom. 6:23; 1 John 5:19; Eph. 2:1, 12; Luke 13:3; Ezek. 18:31, TLB).

In declaring the penalty of sin, God isn't looking for an opportunity to punish people. He doesn't get tough on sin because He wants to get even. To the contrary, He is warning us of a fatal condition: Man's system is poisoned by sin and his survival, happiness, and fulfillment require an antidote.

But there could be only one antidote: blood sacrifice. The law's exacting demands for sacrifices taught graphic lessons about sin's seriousness; lessons that had to be learned, for man's soul was at stake.

Sin is expensive. The second lesson the Law taught is how the payment for sin could be made. In the animal that was brought as a substitutional sacrifice, the Lord provided another picture.

At the time of creation, when God placed a perfect man in a perfect world, He made a contract: "If you sin, death will be the result" (see Gen. 2:17). That contract still stands. That is why sin cannot be ignored or excused—its price is death. But herein lies a problem: If a man pays the price of his sin himself—that is, he dies for his sin—then obviously he will not be present to enjoy the benefits of the price having been paid. So into the dilemma of man's inability to pay his sin's unavoidable debt, the genius of God's plan was introduced: He provided a substitute.

In the lesson book of the original covenant, the substitutes He provided were animals. This temporary plan has created ideological difficulties for those to whom the sacrificial system seems inhumane. But upon closer study, only ignorance or small-mindedness can indict God for insensitivity toward His own creation. The charges that the Old

Testament sacrifices were "so much bloodletting . . . just another ancient cult," do not stand the test of honest investigation.

There is a vast difference between the sacrificial system God gave Moses and the sacrifices of paganism in the ancient world. Given time, pagan ritual inevitably resorted to human sacrifice: children thrown into flames, virgins cast into volcanoes, youths drowned alive to appease demon gods. Paganism's blood sacrifice involved cruelty, superstition, flagellation, and violence.

In contrast, God's lesson plan used animals, insisted on their being killed without cruelty, and dignified humans by divorcing them from superstition. The teaching was a positive stepping-stone toward man's understanding of sacrifice. Consider:

1. The sacrifice was always made mercifully—the creature's death was instantaneous and virtually painless.

2. The sacrifice was not wasted—for the most part, the meat was used as food for both the worshiper and the priest. This is a fact too few realize. There was a joyful feast, celebrating the forgiveness.

3. The sacrifices were readily available, within the resources of all the people—even the poorest could afford the wholly acceptable smaller offerings.

There is no way a thoughtful person can criticize the method God used to teach about substitutionary sacrifice. It was specific and demanding, but it was neither brutal nor loveless. And it *did* teach how the payment for sin would be made.

Still, though the most exacting obedience was rendered,

the lesson-learning did not solve the ultimate problem. Hebrews 9:8 tells us that even in the midst of observing the Law's traditions, there "was never a perfection with regard to the conscience." The regular performance of the sacrifice became a constant reminder that sin still had not been dealt with conclusively. People knew the sacrifice must be repeated next week, next month, next year. And the repetition of the sacrifice was a constant reminder of sin, an inescapable and unforgettable reality "until the time of reformation" (v. 10).

GOD'S REFORMATION

Diorthosis is the New Testament word for reformation. Its central meaning relates to the reordering of something that has been shifted from its original position, or a straightening of something that has been bent, or a mending of something that has been shattered. The cultural use of the word in Bible times further enriches our appreciation of the text, for the same word was used in the medical profession to describe the resetting of a broken or shattered bone; in political circles to describe the setting up of a new kingdom; and in economics to describe the final payment of a debt.

Dramatically, in this one word, Scripture outlines what the ultimate, eternal sacrifice would provide when "the time of reformation" came. Simply summarized, "the reformation" would make possible:

A restructuring of all of man's life;

A straightening of everything warped;

A restoration of life's shattered pieces.

The kingdom of God would bring in a new order of government and make one final payment for man's indebtedness!

And so the traditions led toward the "reformation order," and through their observance mankind was given insight into the forthcoming confrontation with sin that would be faced in man's behalf and fulfilled for man's benefit—by the Visitor.

CHAPTER TEN
THE TRANSACTION
OF THE BLOOD

But this Man, after He had offered one sacrifice for sins forever, sat down at the right hand of God. (Hebrews 10:12)

But this Man. In these three words, our text answers the questions that arose when the reformation was promised: By whom? How? We are told that Christ will transact the redemption of mankind not with the blood of animals, but with His own blood . . . once for all.

Here is a complete transaction, not repeated every year as in the school lessons, but once for all. And by that culminating action, a provision is announced—He has obtained "eternal redemption for us."

In light of our study, these are universe-shaking words!

1. Jesus obtained the eternal redemption of mankind by paying a price—through a single, conclusive transaction;

2. The transaction was accomplished with blood—His own blood, by which means all transgressions under the Law have been covered (vv. 12, 15).

THE RANSOM PAID

In the parlance of the ancient world, *redemption* was a word used in the slave market business. The Greek lexicon defines *redemption* as: "Buying back a slave or captive through the paying of a ransom." Our English dictionary elaborates by defining *ransom* as: "The bringing back of, or release of, a captive or seized property by the payment of money or compliance with other demands." Drama and dynamics unfold in these words—redemption and ransom—as they reveal what the Visitor did for us in the shedding of His blood. For He is "this Man," Christ Jesus, who gave Himself as a ransom for us all (1 Tim. 2:5, 6).

Simply put, Jesus was the ransom paid for man's redemption: His blood was the price paid to recover mankind, the property seized from God's hand. Jesus came into the marketplace of mankind, found slaves on the block, and freed them at the expense of Himself. And He is still coming today to people who are enslaved, hooked in a thousand different ways: Hooked by pride to a never-ending treadmill in pursuit of social acceptance, success, and material possessions; hooked by lust into pursuing the latest trends or easiest relationship, hoping to satisfy the sensuous cravings of debased tastes; hooked by intimidating fears, haunting lies from the past, crushing depression, unceasing pain, or unquenchable hate.

This is the marketplace to which Jesus comes, and it is there that He offers His blood as the ransom payment. And as our "mediator," the one making the transaction, He brings us promise and hope: you can, I can, mankind can . . . we *all* can be unhooked; set free by the payment of

Christ's blood. The payment has already been made, and right now makes possible a new order: a full recovery and complete liberty.

Blood identifies. The meaning of the blood of Jesus is expanded even further when we consider the physical qualities of human blood. For then we find that redemptive applications abound.

First, the word *blood* is a definitive term used in referring to a person's ethnic or social background. For example, when one asks "Where'd your family come from?" or "What's your nationality?" a common answer is "Oh, we're of German blood," or English, African, Oriental, or whatever. So *blood* denotes descent, and due to human prejudices becomes something that often can divide people. The prejudice may be racial or it may be nothing more than family favoritism. "After all," the old saw grinds, "blood runs thicker than water."

Mankind was never intended for such small-hearted, small-minded separatism. When Paul addressed the Athenian philosophers, he said this of God, the Creator of mankind: "He has made from one blood every nation of men" (Acts 17:26). And it's a fact. Though the world is filled with myriad nationalities, languages, cultures, and physical features, the essential sameness and interchangeability of human blood is constant. Although the Bible affirmed this fact long ago, human superstition and prejudice have been ignorant of and resistant to it until relatively recent scientific research validated it.

To this day that physiological fact pictures a spiritual reality, for the blood of Christ is the ultimate unifier. His blood transforms the human heart and produces unity—a social integration that makes all believers "one body," neither slave nor freeman, neither Jew nor Gentile, neither male nor female. This is the way Jesus' blood brings peoples of various races and cultures together: through the love of the Father and the work of the Holy Spirit.

In offering His blood as a covering for people of every nation, Jesus has identified Himself with all mankind, but He paid the price of every man's salvation with blood that is common to every man, regardless of ethnic descent. Therefore, it becomes unsurprising and appropriate that eternal worship will be offered to Jesus by the redeemed from every nation, every kingdom, every tribe, and every tongue. Their unified theme will be the one sacrifice He has made for them and the price paid for their release in a blood common to them all: "Worthy is the Lamb . . . who has washed us with His blood."

Blood verifies. Blood also is often employed as an instrument of verification. Though someone may say in jest, "What do you want, a signature in blood?" the fact remains that documents *have* been signed that way. To this day in some cultures a covenant may be sealed by the cutting of flesh and the intermingling of blood by tribal representatives. It acknowledges a "covenant" and verifies a point of union.

And, though vastly different from primitive ritual, Jesus signed the deed of man's salvation:

He signed the deed with His atoning blood:
He ever lives to make His promise good.
Should all the hosts of hell march in
To make a second claim,
They all march out at the mention of His Name!
They all march out at the mention of His Name!

(Author unknown)

Blood consummates. In his masterpiece of tribute at Gettysburg, Abraham Lincoln employed phrases that are still unforgettable. He referred to those whose blood was shed as having given "the last full measure of devotion," asserting what all recognize: Nothing more consummately declares a full commitment than a man being willing to die for a cause.

Jesus demonstrates that. In shedding His blood voluntarily He testifies to God's absolute commitment to us. In dying, Jesus affirms His full devotion to us. He wasn't forced to die—"No one takes it [my life] from me"—but He chose to die for us (John 10:18).

Now that transaction is accomplished.

The price has been *fully* paid.

I can stand before God with assurance, for my sin has not been swept aside, it has been disannulled.

By the power of Christ's conclusive sacrifice—once for all—my conscience is washed free of sin's guilt and shame. His full measure of devotion has completely settled a new contract. It is established and in force—He's alive and I'm forgiven!

ELEVEN
THE TRANSFUSION
OF THE BLOOD

Transfusion.

The transfer of blood from one person to another.

Transfusion.

The sustaining of the afflicted, sick, or injured.

Through Christ's blood, humankind is afforded a supply of life that frees it to break its dependency on lesser things.

Without the power of Christ's blood within, man may resort to other "power" sources for his system: A spoonful of heroin, a bottle of vodka, a stop at a massage parlor, or some other social joyride, or perhaps a quest for more sophisticated and socially accepted forms of input. Whether respectable or not, in one way or another everyone seems to be crying for "a fix." For the multitude, in fact, does need exactly that—to be fixed. To be put together again.

A more satisfying, durable answer for this need is in a new dimension of living, one with resources and treasure from an inheritance yet untapped—an eternal inheritance (Heb. 9:15). The moment one receives Christ's new life, eternal life begins, and His bequest of an eternal inheritance begins to affect our present circumstance. This blood-bought inheritance involves actual resources. Just as a relative leaves funds, property, or articles of value to help a person improve his present situation, so the blood of Christ provides an instantly available resource to fill life with value and worth. It is that input—that transfusion—which makes deceiving and destructive substitutes not only undesirable, but unnecessary.

Jesus says, "Come to Me. My blood has purchased an inheritance that offers both provision and release; My life to fulfill and free your life."

WHAT BLOOD DOES

In the physical realm, human blood accomplishes three functions:

1. *Blood purifies.* It gathers impurities from various parts of the body and transports them to organs where the purification process takes place.

2. *Blood nourishes.* Food that has been ingested is assimilated into the blood, which carries nourishment to other parts of the body.

3. *Blood helps resist infection.* It contains the cells that resist organisms hostile to the human body.

All three of these functions can be translated into spiritual dynamics when they flow to us through the transfusion of Christ's blood:

1. *Purification through transfusion.* You and I have been born into a race with blood tainted by sin. The Word declares there is a power that flows to us through the blood

of Christ. If we will allow a transfusion of His life into ours, that will set in motion a transformation; an ongoing purification of our lives as "the blood of Jesus Christ His Son cleanses us from all sin" (1 John 1:7).

2. *Nourishment through transfusion.* Jesus said, "Unless you eat the flesh of the Son of Man and drink His blood, you have no life in you" (John 6:53). He interpreted these words by describing them as the teaching of a spiritual truth, not a physical one: The nourishing is real, but it is man's invisible inner being which is fed through Christ's body and blood. He calls us to the Table of Communion, where the composite spiritual truth He taught speaks to us: "This is His body, broken for you . . . and His blood, shed for you. Eat and drink, and a transfusion of His life and power will fill you, to nourish you with strength to meet the challenges of every day."

3. *Resistance through transfusion.* Revelation 12 refers to times like ours when satanic forces attack on every hand. Into that spiritual conflict the Holy Spirit of Truth sends a promise: "They overcame him [the Enemy] by the blood of the Lamb . . ." (v. 11). Here is power to resist the conspiracies of hell, the works of the devil. The legions of darkness are confounded by the blood of Christ. It bewildered them at Calvary, and it will break their stratagems today!

Song of redemption. There is no better way to use the power of Christ's blood to resist the Devil than to sing about it. In concluding this study of the might and miracles in the blood of Christ, I invite you to do so. Sing with me, thinking through what poets and hymnodists have been declaring across the years. The history of the redeemed in Christ is filled with evidence: God has always had a people who understood the power in the blood of Christ. They have written about it magnificently for centuries.

In 1775, Augustus Toplady wrote: "Rock of Ages, cleft for me. Let me hide myself in Thee." The cleft rock is analogous to the slain Lamb—cut open in sacrifice for us. Then, continuing, "Let the water and the blood, from Thy wounded side which flowed, be of sin a double cure: Save from wrath and make me pure."

The dual dynamic of the redemptive transaction is declared: (1) I'm saved from the wrath of judgment, and (2) I'm purified by Christ's life flowing into my life.

In the 1800s, Robert Lowry put it in these words, beginning with a declaration of our absolution from the penalty of past sin:

> What can wash away my sin?
> Nothing but the blood of Jesus.
> What can make me whole again?
> Nothing but the blood of Jesus.

Then Lowry pens the truth of the transforming power of the blood in its present process of bringing us into wholeness:

> O, precious is the flow
> That makes me white as snow,
> No other fount I know,
> Nothing but the blood of Jesus.

This is Edward Mote's nineteenth-century testament:

> My hope is built on nothing less
> Than Jesus' blood and righteousness;
> I dare not trust the sweetest frame,
> But wholly lean on Jesus' Name.

Mote's chorus seems to ignite, exploding with absolute confidence:

> On Christ the solid rock I stand,
> All other ground is sinking sand,
> All other ground is sinking sand.

Another verse from this hymn resounds the certainty of our strength through the blood of Christ:

> His oath, his covenant, his blood,
> Support me in the whelming flood.
> When all around my soul gives way,
> He then is all my hope and stay.

Then, Lewis E. Jones helps us sing of the blood's power to provide an ongoing point of present participation in Jesus' victory:

> Would you be free from your burden of sin?
> There's power in the blood, power in the blood.
> Would you live daily His praises to sing?
> There's wonderful power in the blood.
> There is power, power, wonder-working power,
> In the blood of the Lamb.

There is power, power, wonder-working power,
In the precious blood of the Lamb.

More contemporarily, Andraé Crouch has given us these words:

For it reaches to the highest mountain,
It flows to the lowest valley,
The blood that gives me strength from day to day,
It will never lose its power.

In the blood of Jesus, we have come to the heart of eternal salvation. Its power transcends that one moment of agony two thousand years ago. The blood draining from the Man's body is more than symbolic of a supreme act of love; it is life-begetting today; it is forgiving today; and it is triumphant—today!

Christ's blood penetrates all history. No longer does anyone need to live beneath sin's guilt and condemnation. And no longer do we need to fear the repeated reminders flashed by either our memory or our Enemy. An inheritance of love and power has been bequeathed. A transaction of consummate triumph has been concluded. And because of the blood we have embraced the prospect of life new *in* Him and forever *with* Him.

PART FIVE

HIS DEATH

ALL IS WELL

Raised by hate upon a hill
Stark there stands a cross of wood.
Look, the Man they take and kill,
Is the Lamb, the Son of God.
See the blood now freely flow,
"It is finished," hear Him cry.
Who can understand or know,
Death has won, yet death will die.

Slashing wounds now scar the Lamb,
Blemish-free until He's slain.
Hammer blows into His hand
Thunder forth again, again.
See His body raised in scorn,
See the spear now split His side.
Yet the victory shall be won,
By this Man thus crucified.

Look, the cross now raised on high;
Symbol of Christ's reign above.
Cow'ring demons fear and fly
Driv'n before the flame of love.
All of hell is mystified
Satan thought this hour his gain.
See God's wisdom glorified;
Death destroyed in Jesus' name.

J. W. H.

Inasmuch then as the children have partaken of flesh and blood, He Himself likewise shared in the same, that through death He might destroy him who had the power of death, that is, the devil, and release those who through fear of death were all their lifetime subject to bondage. (Hebrews 2:14, 15)

TWELVE
THE DEATH OF CHRIST

While Christ's resurrection is the most *triumphant* event in history, His death was certainly the most *decisive*. In His dying, Jesus totally altered the power of death forever.

Death does not merely involve the moment a human being takes His last breath. Death is a process of disruptive intrusion into God's original order, set in motion the moment we take our first breath. By reason of man's fall, life has become a relentless process of decay. A fundamental hopelessness resides within most of mankind because of this penalty of man's sin. Death may be rationalized, philosophized, schematized, or ritualized, but inescapably, beyond all humanistic efforts at successfully coping with it, death is realized. Furthermore, the death that inevitably occurs, that of man's certain physical demise, is manifested in many other ways in the details of his lifetime. Death comes in the everyday circumstances and events of our living: visions die, health decays, hopes and dreams fade, relationships wither and often die. A lifetime of dying confronts every man.

But Jesus Christ has come to invade every form of death and to infuse it with His life. He is capable of doing that because in His own dying He absorbed all the power of death in Himself.

In His body, death was swallowed up. In submitting to the torment of Calvary, He mastered the Tormentor. He bore in Himself the full strike of the blade of death and received into Himself all the bitter fruit due to the sinners of the world. Somehow, in one mighty transference, all of the delinquent accounts of the history of human sin and failure were paid by His sinless Person. He received the agony of our penalty and provided the ecstasy of our deliverance.

It is because of His own sinlessness that He was capable of doing this. Only the magnitude of an unencroached-upon, untainted soul could absorb the awesome dimension of sin that Christ encountered on the cross. The sins of the entire human race engulfed Him, but death could not hold Him. In God's Son was found a sinlessness that could take on the guilt of all humanity and still survive an encounter with divine justice. Christ exhausts the power of that sin, breaks the power of death, and comes through in triumph.

The decisiveness of Jesus' death is reflected in the definition it has given to three terms in our language: *crux, crisis,* and *crossroads.*

The crux. *Crux* is the Latin word for cross, and I wonder if we would use that word in common vernacular if it weren't for the fact that the force and impact of the word has been defined by the Cross of the Lord Jesus. We often hear some-

one say, "Get to the *crux* of the matter," meaning "penetrate to the core, bypass the inconsequential." But it seems
the idiom depends on Christ's Cross for definition, for it
was there that the central issues of the human race were
confronted and settled: Sin was paid for and forgiven; death
was faced and banished.

The crisis. *Crisis* is derived from the Greek word for judgment. That's what the Cross was—a place of judgment for
all sin.

Hebrews 9:27 says, "And as it is appointed for men to die
once, but after this the judgment." When He came to that
moment of judgment, Jesus kept an appointment for us:
Our appointment with death as a penalty for sin. That is an
appointment we could never have kept and survived. We
will all keep an appointment with biological death, but we
will never have to withstand the judgment that ordinarily
accompanies it. Why? Because Christ faced it for us. He
bore it all for you and for me. Hallelujah!

So both words, *crux* and *crisis,* seem to derive their primary weight and force from the definition that has been giv-
en to them by the Cross of Christ, on which He dealt with
man's central problem—sin—and vanquished man's central fear—death.

The crossroads. The word *crossroads* indicates a point of
decision, a point where the future is determined. At Calvary
we come to the ultimate crossroads. It is there we face the
most staggering realities this world has ever known:

God's Son died on the Cross;

Man's sin was judged in the Cross;

God's justice was satisfied at the Cross.

Thus, what a person does in the face of Calvary's realities is a conclusive determining factor for every aspect of life—here and hereafter.

God's Son died on the Cross? Don't make the mistake of supposing Jesus to be simply an historic personality, an influential leader, a moral teacher, a gifted prophet, or a dramatic miracle-worker. He is not just a noble martyr who excites admiration through the centuries by His willingness to die for His convictions.

Instead, the significance of the Cross is that the Son of God died there: the only-begotten offspring of the Almighty One of heaven. He is unique; no one like Him has been born before or since. He is specifically, especially, and singly the Savior sent from above, and at the Cross He is executing His purpose in coming and fulfilling the primary reason for His visit here. He who came to share the experience of life *with* us, submitted to death *for* us. "Since we, God's children, are human beings—made of flesh and blood—he became flesh and blood too" (Heb. 2:14, TLB). It was an incredible proposition, but He accepted it, and the Cross of Jesus Christ towers above all history by reason of that primary fact.

Man's sin was judged on the Cross. We discussed earlier how the sin of mankind cannot be lightly dismissed with a wave of the hand. Forgiveness is not easy; sin has to be dealt with. And the forgiveness which has resulted was not easily secured, but it is freely available because His work on the Cross truly and thoroughly dealt with the seriousness of sin.

Sadly, the world has become convinced that the only thing necessary to dispense with sin is for someone to observe a moment of regret, a sincere "I'm sorry." Or many believe that some cosmic largesse should accept the appeal, "Look, so I've failed. Don't be too hard on me. I'm only human."

To man's way of thinking, such appeals should handle the problem of sin.

But sin must be dealt with more seriously and completely because, at the core of the universal structure of things, something has been violated; life is disjointed and disfigured . . . and deadened. Sin is the reason for all of it, and it must be dealt with thoroughly. This need is not because God is vindictive, but because He has lovingly looked upon His fallen race and concluded, "If sin isn't dealt with, they will never be able to enjoy the fulfillment and destiny for which they were created."

In that light we can understand the Cross of Jesus Christ, for that was God's means of dealing with sin. By this one Man, through this one act, God judged sin conclusively: "For as by one man's disobedience many were made sinners, so also by one Man's obedience many will be made righteous" (see Rom. 5:14-19). That obedience was Christ's, and the specific moment of obeying was in His submitting to death on the Cross.

God's justice was satisfied at the Cross. When we speak of God's justice being satisfied in the death of Christ, let us not think it was a matter of God saying, "I need to be appeased," as though He were a vengeful Deity exploding with tantrums until His whims were served. Instead, let's recognize that we're dealing with a God who is the essence of holiness, justice, and righteousness—so much so, that anything contrary to His nature cannot survive the blazing purity of His presence. Yet it is for that presence—that union with Him in intimacy—that He created man. So a dilemma presents itself: The Creator desires the presence and partnership of man, but that creature has fallen from the "like-ness" that allowed for unity in intimacy. The Just One desires the companionship of the one who has unjustly violated trust with Him. He longs for him to return to His side, yet He must insist, "My justice must be satisfied, not because I wish vengeance, but because I cannot change My nature. I cannot be less than just any more than I can be less than loving."

He cannot lie, nor can He use any other means than justice to deal with sin. And the cosmic order is that sin means death to the sinner: "The soul who sins shall die" (Ezek. 18:20).

But the Son is being lifted on Calvary, and whoever believes in Him shall not perish, but shall have eternal life (see John 3:14, 15). Here at the Cross, God is judging sin in an action that will allow Him to embrace man to His heart again: "God so loved the world . . . He gave His only begotten Son"; and the *love* which requires justice miraculously exhausts its wrath on a volunteering substitute: The One Being in the universe able to survive that judgment: Himself . . . His Son.

The Cross destroyed the power of death. But the Cross not only means the victory of forgiveness for sin through God's justice being satisfied. It also provides deliverance from the power sin has to destroy life: "Through death, He . . . [destroyed] him who had the power of death" (Heb. 2:14). The Cross represents a total breakthrough in the entire order of things which bind mankind.

In The Chronicles of Narnia, C. S. Lewis has given us a series of children's stories which beautifully and simply develop the key concepts having to do with spiritual realities. In no way are the stories tedious or preachy, but they run on as a stirring adventure, enticing and entertaining readers of all ages. The opening book, *The Lion, the Witch and the Wardrobe,* is an introduction to the mystical, magical land of Narnia, where animals talk with people, horses fly, and a witch—who is the epitome of evil—lives in conflict with a lion named Aslan. Aslan is clearly meant to symbolize Christ—the Lion of Judah—and Lewis as much as names him "Jesus" before one finishes the seven Narnia volumes. One exchange in the first book states, as clearly as anyone could describe, the destruction of death's power when Jesus died upon the Cross.

Narnia is held in the witch's evil spell of constant winter, and the four children who come to the land seek to break this spell. Edmund, one of the children, has turned traitor against the others and selfishly aligned himself with the witch. The children have earlier warned Edmund against his obvious inclination to side with the witch; but Edmund, like you and me, continues to go against what he knows he ought to be and do and finally sells out to her evil, betraying the other children. Then Edmund's bitter moment of truth arrives. The witch, triumphant in her evil mastery over the boy, confronts Aslan with Edmund's guilt. The other children are looking on:

> "Aslan, you have a traitor there."
>
> "But his offense was not against you."
>
> "But Aslan, have you forgotten the deep magic?" the witch asks.
>
> Aslan answers gravely, "Let us say I *have* forgotten. Tell us of the deep magic."
>
> "Tell you," says the witch, her voice growing suddenly shriller, "tell you what is written in letters as deep as the spear is long in the trunk of the world ash tree? Tell you what is written on the very table of stone which stands beside us? Tell you what is engraved on the scepter of the Emperor beyond the sea? You at least, Aslan, know the magic which the Emperor put into Narnia at the very beginning. You know that every traitor belongs to me as lawful prey, and that for every treachery I have the right to kill."

The witch's statement is a pointed summary of what is true on our planet, of what was written into the very structure of things from the beginning: "In the day that you eat of it you shall surely die" (Gen. 2:17). Death has not come to mankind by mere biological processes, nor does it come at the hands of an angry God. It is the direct result of man's outright disobedience in an act of sin; action which has plunged him into a warped realm that is administrated and directed by "him who had the power of death, that is, the devil" (Heb. 2:14). As seen in Lewis's witch, nothing delights our adversary more than to exact what is his legal right: To administer death to all who have turned against "the Emperor"—the Most High God, the Living One.

To continue the story, Aslan offers himself to the witch in the place of Edmund. As he does, the witch and her lackeys seize Aslan, gleefully bind him with ropes, tear off his mane and brutally slay him.

Susan and Lucy, Edmund's two sisters, watch this scene in horror, unable to believe what has happened. Later, after the witch and her followers are gone, the girls see a legion of small mice swarming over Aslan's lifeless body, chewing at the ropes that bind him to the table. Grief-stricken and overwhelmed with hopelessness, the girls fall asleep. They are awakened by a loud noise and, looking to the stone table on which Aslan was killed, they discover his dead carcass is gone! The ropes which bound him are scattered; the stone on which he was killed is broken. Lucy and Susan are filled with bewilderment until suddenly Aslan appears. As he approaches them, a radiance shines about him, his mane is back and, with every step he takes, flowers rise to blossom in his tracks. The winter spell that held Narnia in its clutches is beginning to thaw and, in the midst of their joyful reunion, one of the girls asks, "Aslan, what does it all mean?"

This is his reply (and the point of the story's retelling): "It means that though the witch knew the deep magic, there is a magic deeper still which she did not know. Her knowledge only goes back until the dawn of time, but if she could have looked a little further back into the stillness and darkness before the dawn of time, she would have read there a different incantation. She would have known that when a willing victim who had committed no treachery was killed in a traitor's stead, the table would crack and death itself would start working backwards."

I know no clearer statement on the significance of the death of Christ. Christianity's finest theologians are surpassed by these words from a children's story. For, simply spoken, Jesus became that willing victim. "For He made Him who knew no sin to be sin for us, that we might become the righteousness of God in Him" (2 Cor. 5:21). And Hebrews 2:14 trumpets that truth: By His death, Jesus destroyed "him who had the power of death," and set the power of death in reverse. The deadening, paralyzing grip of all that clutches and controls us was broken. The yoke which locked life to death-laws has been cast aside, and man's winter of discontent has begun to thaw with the springtime of His deliverance.

THIRTEEN
ALL OUTS, IN FREE

The call of Christ to come into His light harks back to the hide-and-seek game-ender we called out as children: "All the outs, in free."

Of course, ours is more than a children's game of hide and seek. But the fear of being found by God in our sin, or being bound by Satan with our sin, *can* be stopped. His words are life: "If the Son makes you free, you shall be free indeed" (John 8:36).

But the fear of death has closed the door to the light of those words for many "who through fear of death were all their lifetime subject to bondage" (Heb. 2:15). Christ's death delivers us from the fear of death.

We need to define these words *fear of death,* for they address far more than a human shudder at the prospect of dying; more than the fantasy of a screaming descent in a doomed jetliner. The fear of death is not the struggle with a phantom threatening your physical demise. Rather, this phrase describes the devastating sense of hopelessness that often torments us all. The haunting sense that nothing is going to change, that no turnaround will come, that the worst will happen, and that no one will care afterward. There is nothing that gnaws at man's soul more cruelly than this grinding spirit of futility—"the fear of death."

People come to dead-end streets and it is there that they meet death-fear: suffering on a bed of pain, struggling with an ailing marriage, trying to survive a business setback, wondering if the ache of divorce will ever leave.

The same fear sneers when someone doubts whether the tide will turn, if the sun will break through, that the depression will leave, that the habit will be conquered, or if the hurt ever will go away.

When one begins to believe that nothing will ever change, the fear of death has beaten him. Temporarily. Until the message of the deliverance available through Jesus' death gains his trust.

THE CLIMAXING CONQUEST

We have discussed the depths of Christ's love in His condescension, the wholeness we can gain through His suffering, the healing that is available through His wounds, and the forgiveness He provided through His blood.

But the climaxing moment of the hour which He came to fulfill is one of death. And in that action—for it is an action and not merely an occurrence—He drains death of all its power to contain mankind. He is not only paying the penalty of human sin and breaking the bondage imposed by the Serpent's grip, but He is exploding death's power to intimidate, to dictate terms, and to exact tribute.

Because Jesus' body slumped without breath or heartbeat on a cross, death has no more power. He has risen from the tomb and He continues to shout to our generation, "I am alive forevermore and have the keys of hell and death!"

The very fact of His life is the verification that death is a vanquished foe, and in giving His life to us He provides a force in our lives to dominate death in all of its manifestations.

How many live life in a casket of circumstances?

How many tread through life up a gravelike rut?

How many are tangled in the grave clothes of past experiences or habit?

Hear this! To you Christ comes and says, "Fear not! The end of that which has come upon you is near at hand! What you feared would never change is shortly to be overthrown forever!"

My visit with a sufferer. I visited with a friend, an excellent pastor whom I have known since our college days together. A season of frustration had beset him, and in response he had weakened before temptation. His disappointment with himself was exceeded only by his embarrassment at his failure. He left his ministry. He moved his family to another city. He sought solace in the mountains. He bent his back to hard labor in an attempt to forget. He doubted the possibility of ever again realizing what he knew to be his life's God-ordained purpose. Just when it seemed recovery had begun, a new dimension of depression was engulfing him. At this point, he asked if we could get together to talk.

As we conversed, a picture came to my mind: a photograph I sensed to be a God-given scene depicting the condition of his own mind. I saw a pitch-black tunnel, stretching for miles beneath an enormous Everest of a mountain. From the vantage point of my vision, I could see my friend, groping at the front wall of the tunnel, digging his way forward. Tears filled his eyes, evidence of a heart despairing with the belief that the mountain was eternal and the tunnel endless. But the scene I was shown was laden with hope, for only a few feet of the tunnel remained! It was about to end in the breakthrough of blessed daylight and a conclusion of the wearying journey through the darkness.

The scene dissolved, and I looked at my friend and said, "Jim, let me describe your feeling . . . and your thinking." I related the picture, and identified his sense of futility with the prospect that nothing would ever be any different. Then I shared the conclusion: "Jim, there's just a few more feet to go. Don't despair. The Lord is wanting you to know that He has taken all futility out of your life-prospect. Things *will* change. The breakthrough is not far away!"

And Jim wept.

His tears evidenced, at that very minute, a returning, heartwarming confidence as the Spirit of God breathed truth into his soul. After some time, he regained his composure and finally spoke:

"Jack, I don't know how to thank God for those words. The darkness of my soul has been by itself enough to kill hope, but what has been the most destructive to me—robbing my life of any joy—was the thought, 'Nothing will ever change.' But I know that's a lie . . . and God's truth has set me free to believe and to hope with certainty!" It was only a

few weeks until the vision was fulfilled and this man experienced a fresh release in life and light.

But Jim's real release began before he actually experienced it weeks later. It began when he saw the vision of the
Lord's guaranteed victory, and then the fear of death was
broken. His response in faith was not the result of human
wisdom or counsel. It was the Holy Spirit Himself bearing
witness to the greatest truth mankind can ever know: *"Jesus Christ has broken the power of death to rule you at any
point in your life."*

For you who read. You are loved, my friend. And I write you
as a loved one, having no idea what your specific need may
be as you read this book. But whatever it is, I invite you to
come to the Cross of Christ. It is there that Jesus has re-
versed the power of death and brought complete deliverance for you. You no longer need to be trapped, intimidated,
or driven by the things resulting from past or present bondage.

He loves you with an everlasting love.

And because that everlasting love reaches out *right now*
to meet you at *any* point in your life, I issue this gentle invi-
tation. I invite you to bring that point of problem, that sting
of stress, or that agony of bondage which most troubles you
now. With your prayerful imagination, take it in hand and
place it at the foot of the Cross. Wait there and let the light of
His everlasting love and almighty triumph shine on it.
Speak your heart openly to Him. If you wish, use the prayer
I have written for you below, inserting your points of heart-

felt need—as many as you wish. As you do so, pour your heart out before Him in a simple, childlike way. The Visitor is drawing near right now . . . visiting you again at your point of suffering with the resources of His triumph over every pain, every wound, all suffering, bondage, and death.

Speak to Him.

A PRAYER OF RECEIVING

Father, I bring You . . . (insert *your* heart's cry) that the bonds may be broken.

I bring You . . . (speak to Him *your* need) that the victory You offer may be realized.

I bring my fears, my loneliness, and my doubts . . . (name them).

I renounce any bitterness that I may have entertained in my heart. (Admit to it without fear of reprisal. Confession brings release.)

Jesus, You were *pierced through* that I might have a *breakthrough*. Release me, dear Lord, as I receive Your freedom, healing, and deliverance, right now. Amen.

A PRAYER OF PRAISEFUL COMMITMENT

Jesus, thank You for coming to visit me, for suffering for me, for Your wounds in my behalf, for Your blood securing my deliverance, and for Your Cross destroying death's fearsome power. Thank You that You have done this all for me, and I bow with thanks—bringing my praise, my worship, and my life given back, all to You. Amen.

A FRIDAY'S REMEMBRANCE

This day I come to celebrate
The day You died to consecrate
A race forlorn;
Which, 'til You came,
Was without hope or champion.

You came—what incongruity!
God is man;
Eternity's confined to time
That men might be
Renewed to live in dignity.

To reconcile, a battle plan
Is laid to purchase peace.
You spanned
The chasm carved by human sin;
Your Cross-quake
closed the breach between.

That Friday has named this one "Good."
How can it be?
We spilled Your blood!
What guilt!
Yet "Good," I hear You say,
"My new creation birthed this day."

While birth pangs break Your body there,
On Calvary, my stripes You wear.
Your wounded hands,
Your heart,
Your side
Are flowing, Lord, a healing tide.

And so this day's remembrance
Remembering, remembering:

The cost,
The Cross,
The Christ—God's Son.
Lord Jesus, it's to You I come.

I come to take, I come to drink
Again of grace,
And here I think
What great salvation You afford:
I've been redeemed,
Returned,
Restored!

I live again because You died,
Partake the feast Your love provides;
I break Your body,
Take Your Blood,
While seated at Your table, Lord.

This leper—clean!
This blind man sees!
Your Cross the doubly healing Key
Now freeing me from death's decay;
Now flooding life with endless day.

J. W. H.